Women's Figures

An Illustrated Guide to the Economic Progress of Women in America

2012 Edition

Diana Furchtgott-Roth

AEI Press

Publisher for the American Enterprise Institute
Washington, D.C.

Distributed to the Trade by National Book Network, 15200 NBN Way, Blue Ridge Summit, PA 17214. To order call toll free 1-800-462-6420 or 1-717-794-3800. For all other inquiries please contact the AEI Press, 1150 Seventeenth Street, N.W., Washington, D.C. 20036 or call 1-800-862-5801.

Library of Congress Cataloging-in-Publication Data

Furchtgott-Roth, Diana.
Women's figures : an illustrated guide to the economic progress of women in America / Diana Furchtgott-Roth.—2nd ed.
    p. cm.
    Includes bibliographical references and index.
    ISBN 978-0-8447-7241-7 (cloth)—ISBN 0-8447-7241-0 (cloth)—ISBN 978-0-8447-7242-4 (pbk.)—ISBN 0-8447-7242-9 (pbk.)—ISBN 978-0-8447-7243-1 (ebook)—ISBN 0-8447-7243-7 (ebook)
    1. Women—United States—Economic conditions—20th century—Statistics. 2. Sex discrimination in employment—United States—History—20th century—Statistics. 3. Sex discrimination against women—United States—History—20th century—Statistics. I. American Enterprise Institute for Public Policy Research. II. Independent Women's Forum (Organization) III. Title.
HQ1426.F885 2012
305.40973—dc23

                                                                    2011048723

Printed in the United States of America

For Harold, who still appreciates my figure.

Table of Contents

Acknowledgments

*T*his book would not have been completed without the help of many people. I would like first to thank Barbara Ledeen, who conceived the idea for the book and its title, in 1996. The original *Women's Figures*, coauthored with Christine Rosen (then Christine Stolba), was published in 1999 by the AEI Press and the Independent Women's Forum.

I am grateful to my colleagues at the Manhattan Institute for Policy Research, especially Larry Mone and Howard Husock, for their support of this project. In addition, my colleagues at Hudson Institute, including Irwin Stelzer, Kenneth Weinstein, Herbert London, John Weicher, and Lewis Libby, provided invaluable advice and comments. Astha Shrestha, Amlan Banerjee, Zohara Levine, Ivana Stosic, Joshua Sheppard, and Claire Rogers provided help with research and frequent data updates as the book progressed.

My friends at AEI, where I was a resident fellow for many years, gave me many helpful suggestions. Christina Hoff Sommers, Mark Perry, Karlyn Bowman, and Christopher DeMuth were instrumental in developing and expanding the book. Professor June O'Neill of Baruch College, City University of New York, and Arlene Holen of the Technology Policy Institute provided invaluable comments.

I would like to thank the Searle Freedom Trust and Kim Dennis, its President and Chief Executive Officer, for research support.

List of Illustrations

Figures

Tables

List of Abbreviations

AAUW	American Association of University Women
BLS	Bureau of Labor Statistics
CAWP	Center for American Women and Politics
CBO	Congressional Budget Office
CPS	Current Population Survey
CWBR	Center for Women's Business Research
ERA	Equal Rights Amendment
GAO	Government Accountability Office
NCES	National Center for Education Statistics
NOW	National Organization for Women
NWLC	National Women's Law Center
OECD	Organisation for Economic Co-operation and Development
SBA	Small Business Association
SRAT	Gender Stereotype Risk Assessment Toolkit
STEM	Science, Technology, Engineering, and Mathematics

INTRODUCTION

Introduction

*C*onventional wisdom holds that women suffer from discrimination in the workplace that leaves them economically worse off than men. The American Association of University Women (AAUW) asserts that "women have made remarkable strides in education during the past three decades, but these gains have yet to translate into full equity in pay—even for college-educated women who work full time."[1] According to Kim Gandy, President of the National Organization for Women (NOW), "the jury is in, the studies are done, and the conclusions are consistent: the gender pay gap is alive and well. The disparity between what women and men are paid stubbornly persists, even after controlling for years of education, work experience and type of occupation."[2]

Yet compared to men, women in twenty-first-century America live five years longer; face a lower unemployment rate; earn a substantially larger share of high school diplomas, associate's, bachelor's, and master's degrees; and face lower rates of incarceration, alcoholism, and drug abuse. When women and men in the same jobs and with the same experience are compared, the wage gap disappears. In other words, contrary to what AAUW, NOW, and many other women's groups would have Congress believe, women are doing well.

Unfortunately, the myth of women as victims persists. President Obama and many in Congress advocate policies that favor women over men. For example, the Dodd-Frank financial regulation law has mandated 29 offices for the advancement of women. The Patient Protection and Affordable Care Act has established multiple offices of women's health. President Obama is weighing quotas for women in university science and math programs like the quotas in place for women in university sports.

Much of this is motivated by congressional defensiveness in the face of fierce, and largely unopposed, lobbying by women's groups. Previously, women's rights advocates pressed for equality of opportunity. Now that has been largely achieved, they clamor for equal outcomes—a result that a prudent Congress would refrain from trying to achieve through legislation. Equal outcomes is a pernicious goal for government policy, one that smacks of central planning and heavy official intrusion into private decisions including what to study academically and what vocation to pursue.

Women as a group spontaneously make choices that are different from men's, and there is nothing wrong with their freely making such choices. Women's groups that attempt to shape other women's choices through government policies would put themselves out of business were they to acknowledge the validity of free choice.

By lobbying for equality of opportunity, feminists in the 1960s and 1970s were rightly sending the message that women can take care of themselves in the economy and in society. Helen Reddy's song "I Am Woman," top of the charts in 1972, contained the lyrics "I am strong, I am invincible, I am woman." Helen Reddy's woman was not intimidated by going into law or medicine, and the idea that she would need affirmative action and quotas to go into science or finance contradicts the basic message that women are as strong as men.

In contrast, the twenty-first-century feminist message is that women are weak and need protection through special preferences. Not only does this harm men by depriving them of opportunities, it harms women by undermining their hard-earned credentials. Even a feminist might hesitate to choose a female surgeon for delicate surgery if she knew that the surgeon had been hired under an affirmative action program. Instead, the patient would choose a male who might be the better surgeon. Giving preferences to a few women sows seeds of doubt that reflect on all women.

The irony is that women succeed in everyday America, but many in Washington argue that women will be doomed to failure unless they receive preferential treatment. Of course, this arises from a distorted view of failure in official Washington. A woman who chooses a part-time job with a flexible schedule in order to have time both for family and career thinks of herself as successful. But to many women's groups and government leaders in Washington, she is a failure because she is on a lower earnings path than most men and she is not on track to be a chief executive.

Many continue to claim that government intervention in the workplace and broader economy is necessary if women are to achieve equality with men. However, a closer examination shows that these claims are based on false premises about women and their economic successes. Indeed, women in the United States have made real progress over the past half-century in many areas including education, entrepreneurship, the military, science, and law enforcement agencies.

This book challenges misconceptions about women's progress and provides examples of how women continue to become ever closer to men in terms of their educational, career, and earnings prospects.

Chapter 1 discusses the supposed 23 percent gender wage gap and the misguided policy proposals that aim to address the purported, but now negligible, problem of wage discrimination. Chapter 2 describes women's educational attainment and choices, focusing on the high female graduation rates from high school and college, as well as on differences between men's and women's choices of majors. Chapter 3 shows how the marriage penalty, our tax system, and Social Security discourage women from working and thus contribute to lower lifetime earnings for women. Chapter 4 describes the increasing numbers of women among America's entrepreneurs and examines reasons some women find entrepreneurship attractive. Chapter 5 compares the progress of African American, Hispanic American, and Asian American women in achieving economic equality with men of the same racial background, and it also makes comparisons between these minority women's progress and white women's progress. Chapter 6 shows how American women compare with their counterparts abroad in terms of labor force participation, employment, fertility, and educational attainment. Chapter 7 discusses the political machine that lobbies for more preferences for women even in light of women's many successes. Chapter 8 offers conclusions and implications for policy.

NOTES

1. "The Gender Pay Gap." American Association of University Women, http://www.aauw.org/learn/research/statedata/ (accessed September 8, 2011).

2. Kim Gandy. "On Equal Pay Day NOW Calls Attention to Persistent Gender Wage Gap." National Organization for Women press release, http://www.now.org/press/04-09/04-27.html (accessed September 12, 2011).

PART I

Facts and Myths about Women at Work and in Politics

*W*omen today have nearly closed the formerly wide divisions that separated men and women in terms of economic and social status. This chapter examines labor force participation, the narrowing gaps in wages, occupational choices, and election to public office. In spite of these achievements, women are often perceived as suffering from discrimination that causes them to earn lower wages and excludes them from certain occupations as well as from attaining leadership positions in businesses and public offices. These misperceptions are undermined by full analyses of the choices women make that bear on their career and life paths, and by due attention to the successes women have achieved.

Women's Labor Force Participation Rates and Unemployment

The labor force participation rate is comprised of those who are employed and unemployed as a percent of the working age population. Those who are in the working-age population and who have a job or are currently looking for one are counted as part of the labor force; people who are not looking for employment are not part of the labor force. The labor force participation rate for women rose steadily from 43 percent in 1970 to 60 percent in the late 1990s, as shown in figure 1-1. Women moved into the labor force in response

FIGURE 1-1

Percentage of Women Who Work, 1970–2011

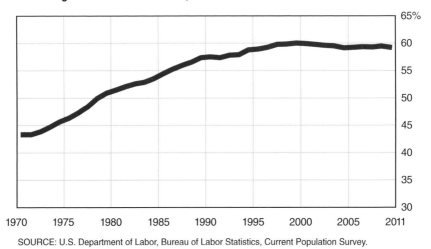

SOURCE: U.S. Department of Labor, Bureau of Labor Statistics, Current Population Survey.

FIGURE 1-2

Women's Share of the Labor Force, 1970–2011

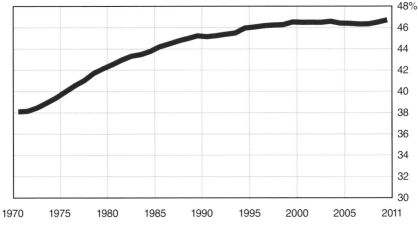

SOURCE: U.S. Department of Labor, Bureau of Labor Statistics, Current Population Survey.

to increased opportunities, and found jobs in a wide range of professions. Figure 1-2 shows that women make up around 47 percent of the total labor force, a figure that has remained quite stable since 1999. The continuous rise of the labor force participation rate until

FIGURE 1-3

FIGURE 1-3

Total Employment by Sex, 1970–2011

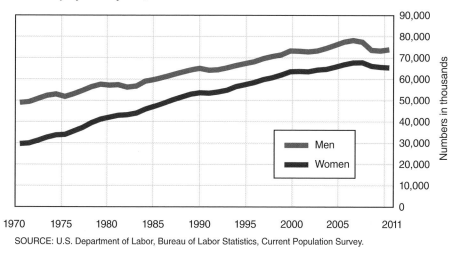

SOURCE: U.S. Department of Labor, Bureau of Labor Statistics, Current Population Survey.

FIGURE 1-4

Full-time Employment by Sex, 1970–2011

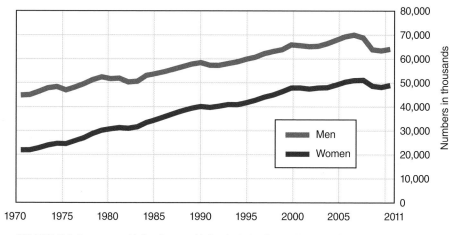

SOURCE: U.S. Department of Labor, Bureau of Labor Statistics, Current Population Survey.

2000 reflected the increased educational achievement of women in the United States. Since the late 1990s, the labor force participation rate has declined to 58 percent. The largest decline occurred during and following the recession of 2008–2009, which eliminated many

FIGURE 1-5

Part-time Employment by Sex, 1970–2011

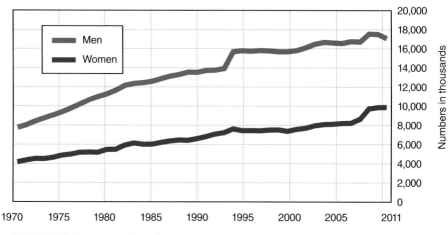

SOURCE: U.S. Department of Labor, Bureau of Labor Statistics, Current Population Survey.

opportunities. Additionally, it appears that some women have gone back to prioritizing family over work.[1]

Since 1970, the number of female workers has increased by approximately 30 million to around 66 million, as shown in figure 1-3. Figures 1-4 and 1-5 confirm that the increase in the number of employed women has been in both full-time and part-time occupations. The increase in the number of full-time female employees has risen by almost 29 million since 1970, and the number of part-time female employees rose by about 6 million. Such optimistic trends clearly contradict claims by critics such as legal scholar Deborah Rhode, who argue that women are "trapped in part-time positions."[2] While technological innovation helped women spend more time at work over the course of the twentieth century,[3] the rise in availability of child care has undoubtedly made it even easier for mothers to choose employment.[4] It is, therefore, not a surprise that the difference in labor force participation rates of married and unmarried women is a mere 1.3 percent, as shown in figure 1-6.

Figure 1-7 shows that male and female unemployment rates, after moving together for the past three decades, have diverged in favor of women. In 2010, women's unemployment rates were almost

FIGURE 1-6

Women's Labor Force Participation Rates by Marital Status, 1970–2011

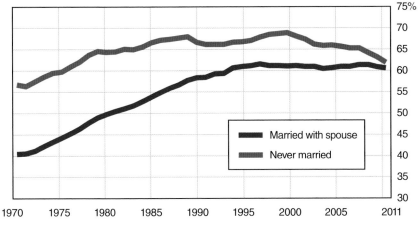

SOURCE: U.S. Department of Labor, Bureau of Labor Statistics, Current Population Survey.

FIGURE 1-7

Unemployment Rates by Sex, 1970–2011

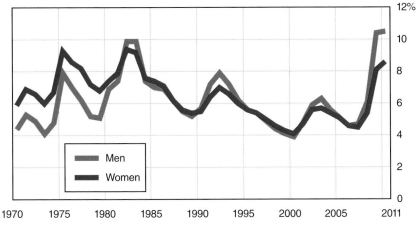

SOURCE: U.S. Department of Labor, Bureau of Labor Statistics, Current Population Survey.

two percentage points below men's and they remained lower when this volume went to press. If discrimination persisted, and women were not hired as a result, unemployment rates of women would have been higher than those of men.

FIGURE 1-8

Distribution of Women's Labor Force by Educational Attainment, 1970–2010 (Aged 25 to 64 Years)

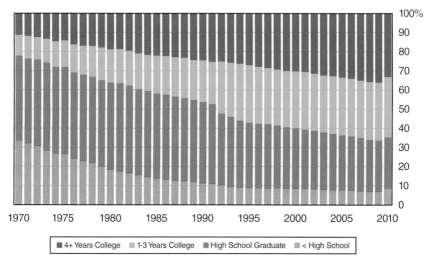

SOURCE: U.S. Department of Labor, Bureau of Labor Statistics, *Women in the Labor Force: A Databook* (2010), table 9.

Not only are more women participating in the workforce, but they are taking jobs that require higher degrees of education, as demonstrated in figure 1-8. Until 2001, high school graduates made up the highest percentage of the women's labor force (aged 25 to 64 years). The percentage of women in the labor force with only a high school education is declining steadily, now down to below 30 percent from about 42 percent as recently as 1990. Similarly, the percentage of the women's labor force that has less than a high-school education is now at 7 percent and continues to decline. By 2010, college graduates made up the highest percentage at 33 percent, followed by women who have had one to three years of college education at 32 percent. In 1970, college graduates made up 11 percent. Over 65 percent of the female labor force has at least one year of college education, compared with 23 percent in 1970. The changes in the composition demonstrate that the labor market has been providing an increasing number of opportunities for educated and skilled women.

The Myth of the "Wage Gap"

Women are often said to suffer from a "wage gap"—the difference between the wages women and men earn.

For the decade between 1980 and 1990, the wage gap between women and men decreased steadily, as shown in figure 1-9. Although the gap between women's and men's wages was stable for the decade of 1993-2003, it has again been closing in the years since 2003. The U.S. Department of Labor's Bureau of Labor Statistics finds that women on average earned 80 cents for every dollar that men earned in 2008 and 2009, using full-time median weekly earnings.[5] The U.S. Census Bureau similarly reports that the 2009 ratio of women's earnings to men's earnings was 78 cents to the dollar, using full-time median annual earnings.[6] However, these numbers do not represent the compensation of women compared to men in specific jobs, because they average all male and female full-time employees, rather than comparing men and women in the same jobs with the same experience.

FIGURE 1-9

Women's Median Usual Weekly Earnings as a Percentage of Men's, 1979–2011

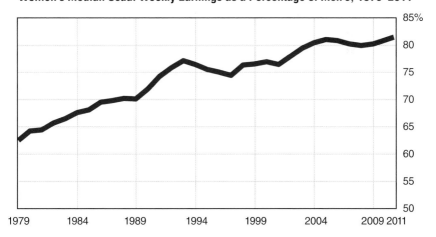

SOURCE: U.S. Department of Labor, Bureau of Labor Statistics, *Women in the Labor Force: A Databook* (2010), table 16; *Employment and Earnings* (January 2010), annual averages, table 37.

If we compare wages of men and women who work forty hours a week, without accounting for any differences in jobs, training, or time in the labor force, Labor Department data show the wage ratio decreases to 87 percent.[7] Marriage and children explain some of the wage gap, because many mothers value flexible schedules. In 2010 single women working full-time earned 97 percent of men's earnings, but married women earned merely 77 percent, even before accounting for differences in education, jobs, and experience.

When the wage gap is analyzed by individual occupations, job and employee characteristics, regional labor markets, job titles, job responsibilities, and employee experience, the wage gap shrinks even more. When these differences are considered, many studies show that men and women make about the same. For instance, a 2009 study by the economics consulting firm CONSAD Research Corporation, published by the U.S. Department of Labor, shows that women make 94 percent of what men make.[8] The remaining 6 percent is due to unexplained variables, only one of which might be discrimination.

In a similar vein, a 2007 report by the Congressional Research Service states that "although these disparities between seemingly comparable men and women sometimes are taken as proof of sex-based wage inequities, the data has not been adjusted to reflect gender difference in all characteristics that can legitimately affect relative wages (for instance, college major or uninterrupted years of employment)."[9] As University of Massachusetts economist Randy Albelda has testified, once those factors are taken into account, the gap shrinks considerably.[10]

Dozens of studies on the gender wage gap that attempt to measure "discrimination" have been published in academic journals in the past several decades.[11] Unlike the Bureau of Labor Statistics, which uses simple mathematical tools to calculate the wage ratio, these studies use an econometric technique called regression analysis to measure how much various factors each contribute to the wage gap. The residual that cannot be explained by any of the included variables is frequently termed "discrimination." Many of these studies suffer from a problem called omitted variable bias, which means that they fail to include enough explanatory variables to account truly for all, or even most, of the factors that plausibly affect wages.[12] Thus, studies that omit variables that are germane to differences between women's and men's workforce experiences are apt to find a large amount of "discrimination."

However, an increase in the number of explanatory variables in a regression analysis significantly reduces the residual portion attributable to "discrimination." For example, economist June O'Neill of the City University of New York showed that the adjusted wage ratio between men and women in 2000 increased from 78 percent to 97 percent when appropriate explanatory variables were included in calculations. She found that when she included data about demographics, education, scores on the Armed Forces Qualification Test, and work experience, the wage ratio increased to 91 percent. When workplace and occupation characteristics, as well as child-related factors, were added, the wage ratio rose to 95 percent. Finally, when she included data about the percentage of women in the occupation, such as teacher or manager, the wage ratio increased to 97 percent.[13]

In another study, June and Dave O'Neill argue that the gender pay gap arises from women's choices on "the amount of time and energy devoted to her career, as reflected in years of work, experience, utilization of part-time work, and other workplace and job characteristics." They base their findings on detailed study of the extent to which non-discriminatory factors explain wage gaps.[14]

Similarly, Marianne Bertrand of the University of Chicago and Kevin Hallock of Cornell University found an insignificant difference in the pay of male and female top corporate executives when factoring in the size of the firm, company position, age, seniority, and tenure. They found that accounting for detailed occupation causes the female-to-male wage ratio to rise from 56 percent to 87 percent, and that accounting for age and tenure causes the wage ratio to jump from 56 percent to 95 percent.[15]

Moreover, many studies on the pay gap ignore the fringe benefits given to workers that account for approximately one-third of total compensation. University of Michigan economist Helen Levy, formerly a member of the White House's Council of Economic Advisors, found that the gap in health insurance coverage, 8.8 percent, was only half as large as the pay gap, 25 percent. Thus, using both health insurance and wages rather than using wages alone would result in a smaller estimate of the gender pay gap.[16]

Finally, experimental psychology shows that women's preferences are different from men's. Economists Rachel Corson of the University of Texas at Dallas and Uri Gneezy of the University of California, San Diego, reviewed experimental studies on behavior and found that women and men have significant differences in preferences when it comes to risk-taking, social preferences, and competition.[17] In behavioral experiments, women are more risk-averse, less competitive, and more sensitive to subtle social cues than men, leading them to choose professions with less risk-taking, fewer degrees of competition, and flexible careers. These behaviors might translate into lower pay and slower advancement within their chosen professions.[18]

Along the same vein, a 2009 study published by the U.S. Government Accountability Office (GAO) found that "all but about 7 cents of the gap can be explained by differences in measurable factors such as the occupations of men and women and, to a lesser extent, other factors such as education levels and years of federal experience."[19]

Perhaps the most obvious difference in behavior between men and women is that the latter give birth. As discussed in the next section, women's choices regarding motherhood can affect their earnings. A study by Jane Waldfogel found an overall female to male wage ratio of 0.84, which rose to 0.95 when the wage ratio was calculated as childless women to men.[20]

The *Myth* of the "*Mother's Penalty*"

Some have alleged discrimination as the cause of a gap in earnings between women with children and those without. Official labor statistics, graphed in figure 1-10, do indicate a higher wage gap for women with children than for those without children, as mothers tend to have lower wages than women without children, all other factors being equal. This is widely known as the "mother's penalty," and many argue that it exists because of discrimination. However, as

FIGURE 1-10

Gender Wage Ratio by Presence and Age of Children, 2010

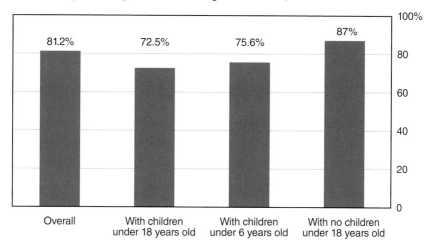

SOURCE: U.S. Department of Labor, Bureau of Labor Statistics, *Highlights of Women's Earnings in 2009* (2010).

with the "wage gap," various empirical findings prove that it is more a matter of productivity and preference than discrimination. Nonetheless, feminist groups argue that government intervention must help eradicate not only the persistent inequality between men and women, but also inequality between women with children and those without.

These women's groups allege that the gaps in earnings between mothers and women without children at home is caused by discrimination women suffer not only in the workplace but at home. For example, the American Association of University Women (AAUW) addresses purported discrimination at home in its study *Behind the Pay Gap*. Noting that the majority of parenting responsibilities fall on mothers rather than fathers, the AAUW writes that "women's personal choices are…fraught with inequities."[21] This statement suggests that women make choices that are not in their best interests. The AAUW ascribes this problem to the so-called "social construction" of gender roles. However, gender roles are determined not entirely by nurture but also by nature. For example, after a birth, it is the mother, not the father, who needs time to rest and to recover. Even if the social construction of gender roles were eliminated, women would need leave from work that men would not.

Moreover, mothers value time with their children, and many mothers choose flexible jobs and to work fewer hours to be able to spend more time with their family. The late historian Elizabeth Fox-Genovese wrote "even highly successful women frequently want to spend much more time with their young children than the sixty-hour weeks required by the corporate fast tracks will permit."[22]

Fox-Genovese's claim is substantiated by economists Claudia Goldin and Lawrence Katz of Harvard University and Marianne Bertrand of the University of Chicago, who report that the presence of children was the major reason behind career interruptions and fewer working hours of the female MBA graduates they studied. They found that, although all MBA graduates entered the job market with the same amount of compensation for the same jobs, over the years women's pay may have lagged behind men's because of differences in working hour and career choices.[23]

It is noteworthy that the past three female nominees for U.S. Supreme Court Justice, Sonia Sotomayor, Elena Kagan, and Harriet Miers (who later withdrew), have no children, and could devote themselves completely to their careers.

Nevertheless, many organizations like the AAUW and the National Organization for Women (NOW) are quick to attribute the unexplained portion of the pay gap to discrimination. For example, the AAUW study *Behind the Pay Gap* mentioned above shows that even when all various factors normally associated with pay have been included in the computation, the wage gap persists. The AAUW attributes this to gender discrimination.[24] But its study relies on a narrow and simplistic interpretation of the pay gap that ignores the complexity of the issue at hand and the reasons why women's spontaneous choices may result in a pay gap.

With so many plausible explanations for the gap in compensation between women and men, it is simply irrational to argue that it exists because of "persistent discrimination." However, as narrowing gaps in pay rates reflect increasing similarity in the characteristics of workers in terms of jobs, educational attainment, and level of experience, documented in the 2009 GAO report referenced in table

TABLE 1-1

Comparisons of Literature on Gender Wage Gap

Researcher	Year	Sample From	Factors Included in Adjusted Ratio	F/M Wage Ratio	
				Unadjusted	Adjusted
Jane Waldfogel	1989	Population	Age, Gender, Race, Education, Hourly Wage, Work Experience, Marital Status, Number of Children	0.84	**0.95**
Bertrand and Hallock	2001	Top Executives, Managers	Industrial Specialization, Firm Size, Average Weekly Earnings of Workers Working over 35 Hours, Compensation, Age and Tenure of Manager	0.56	**0.95**
June O'Neill	2003	Population	Age, Gender, Race, Education, SMSA, Region, AFQT, Work Experience, Time Lost Due to Family Responsibilities, Class of Worker, Occupational Characteristics, Percent Female in Occupation	0.78	**0.97**
BLS	2008	Population	Full-Time Weekly Wages of Workers Who Work 40 Hours per Week	0.8	**0.87**
Census Bureau	2009	Population	Full-Time Annual Wages	0.78	-
GAO	2009	Federal Workers	Breaks in Federal Service, Unpaid Leave, Education, Occupational Differences, Federal Experience, Worker Characteristics	0.89	**0.93**

NOTE: The unadjusted wage ratio includes compensation only.

For the wage ratios provided in Jane Waldfogel's study, 0.84 is the overall female to male wage ratio and 0.95 is the wage ratio of non-mothers to male.

1-1,[25] it has become clear that the American workplace is meritocratic. Yet the allegations of discrimination continue, even though, under current law, it is possible for workers to sue employers if they believe discrimination has occurred. Today American women have the same opportunities as men in the workplace. But often, they make different choices.

Government interventions targeted against discrimination will not close the pay gap if women's spontaneous choices about education, career, and family are the true causes of the gaps in pay. However, supporters of the discrimination theory have kept pushing bills such as the Fair Pay Act of 2011 as well as additional government regulations.[26] These regulations have a high potential to harm rather than to help women. For example, in order to escape pay guidelines, employers may actually find it easier to hire men than women. Rather than trying to protect women from discrimination that has almost disappeared, it would be better to acknowledge that many women chose career paths different from those of most men—with the confidence that those women who do want the "corner office" will be able to earn it, as discussed in the next section.

The Myth of the "Glass Ceiling"

Like the "wage gap" and the "mother's penalty," the notion of the "glass ceiling" has been widely accepted as fact. Coined in the 1980s by the *Wall Street Journal*, this catchy phrase is defined as an "invisible but impenetrable barrier between women and the executive suite."[27] Proponents of the existence of the glass ceiling assert that women are systematically excluded from opportunities for advancement to higher-level management and leadership roles. They point to the underrepresentation of women in top corporate roles as evidence of discrimination against female candidates. However, underrepresentation alone is weak evidence, for if we look closely at women's career paths we find very different reasons behind the low numbers of women in top jobs.

Proponents of the existence of a glass ceiling include the U.S. Department of Labor, which established a Glass Ceiling Commission that was in existence from 1991 to 1996. The Glass Ceiling Commission began with the premise that there is a glass ceiling for women in corporate America. The Commission released an ominous report in 1995, which stated that only 5 percent of senior managers at Fortune 1000 and Fortune 500 service companies were women. However, this 5 percent figure was calculated using a biased methodology. Rather than calculating the percentage of senior management positions awarded to women out of the total pool of men and women qualified for these roles—say, the number of working men and women who have an MBA with at least 25 years of work experience—it calculated this percentage of senior management positions awarded to women out of the total labor force. Many more women were entering corporate jobs in 1995 than 25 years earlier, so by 1995 few women had reached the top of the corporate ladder.

It is surprising that the Glass Ceiling Commission did not take this into account, given its attention to "preparedness" of women and minorities to rise to top corporate positions and their attention to the "corporate pipeline." The Commission assumed that a leadership candidate must be "in the pipeline" long enough to gain the necessary experience and skills before qualifying for top executive jobs. It is not difficult to realize that very few women entered the pipeline in the 1960s and 1970s. Only a few graduated with professional degrees and even fewer remained in the workforce long enough to garner the necessary experience, which explains why the Commission found there was a dearth of women executives in 1995. Figure 2-3 shows the percent of MBA degrees awarded to women between 1970 and 2009. Given that top corporate jobs require one to be in the pipeline for at least 25 years, fewer than 5 percent of the qualified candidates for these jobs were women in 1995.

Even today, and even on the assumption that all female MBA recipients had been active in business careers since graduation, fewer than 25 percent of those qualified for executive jobs would be women. Given that in 2009, roughly half, or about 45 percent, of MBA degrees were awarded to women, we cannot expect the pipeline to deliver roughly equal number of qualified men and women until after 2030—provided as high a fraction of female as male MBA graduates remain active in their business careers. Critics who are appalled by the systems' unequal gender distribution of top managerial and executive positions should consider these statistics before jumping to conclusions.

The Glass Ceiling Commission report noted that "certain functional areas are more likely than others to lead to the top. The 'right' areas are most likely to be line functions such as marketing and production or critical control functions such as accounting and finance."[28] The report also concluded that certain factors are necessary to climb the corporate ladder. These include broad and varied experience in the core areas of business; access to information, particularly through networks and mentoring; company seniority; initial job assignment; high job mobility; education; organizational savvy; long hours and hard work; and career planning.[29] The Commission's report argued that there are barriers to women within the pipeline that restrict women's access to the networks, mentors, assignments, and other keys to success that slow women's progress to senior positions.

More recent studies have found that women are making their way into top management in increasing numbers. For example, the Korn/Ferry executive search firm reports that by 2007, women were represented in 85 percent of the Fortune 1000 boards, up from 78 percent in 2001, 53 percent in 1988, and 11 percent in 1973. In 2010, women were represented on 97 percent of Korn/Ferry's Market Cap 100 boards, a new measure.[30]

Consistent with the Korn/Ferry findings, the U.S. General Accountability Office (GAO) found that in 2000, half of the ten industries studied had no statistically significant difference between the percent of management positions filled by women and the percent of all industry positions filled by women. In almost all the industries where the difference was significant—namely, educational services, retail trade, finance, insurance and real estate, hospitals and medical services, and professional medical services—the majority of management positions were filled by women. The only exception was retail trade, where men still had an advantage. Still, the GAO found that, while women in management have been attaining increasingly similar levels of education and work characteristics as men, significant differences still remain: female managers had less education, were younger, were more likely to work part-time, and were less likely to be married than men in management.[31]

As discussed above, these differences can be explained by noting that women have different preferences, are more likely to work part-time, and also tend to take more career breaks, which leads them to accumulate less work experience. Such factors that become "barriers" to upward mobility at work are the same reasons behind the gender wage gap—but are nevertheless freely chosen by women in order to balance work and family responsibilities.

FIGURE 1-11

Women as a Percentage of Total Employment by Occupation, 1983, 1997, and 2010

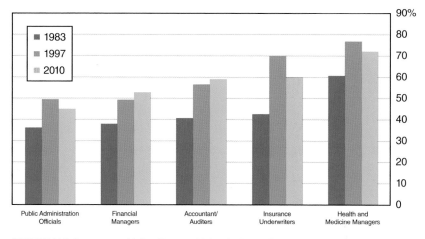

SOURCE: U.S. Department of Labor, Bureau of Labor Statistics, *Employment and Earnings* (January 2011). Unpublished tabulations from *Current Population Survey*.

The trend is for women to move into the jobs that may take many of them into top management: by 2010, as shown in figure 1-11, women made up the majority of jobs in financial managing, accounting and auditing, insurance underwriting, and health and medicine managing. This evidence highlights women's achievements in the workplace and casts further doubt on discrimination theory.

The Myth of the "Pink Ghetto"

The phrase "pink ghetto," potent in invoking connotations of stereotypes, poverty, inequality, and powerlessness, refers to the gender differences in occupation as a result of segregation. Just as some believe in a wage gap, a mother's penalty, and a glass ceiling, it is alleged that many women workers are trapped in a "pink ghetto."

"If more than half the population is denied access to 60 percent of the occupations, being crowded into a few at lower earnings,

TABLE 1-2

Selected Occupations with Less than 10 Percent Women, 2010

Occupations	Share of Women Employed
Automotive service technicians and mechanics	1.8
Bus and truck mechanics and diesel engine specialists	0.3
Carpenters	2.2
Construction laborers	2.1
Crane and tower operators	0.0
Driver/sales workers and truck drivers	3.3
Electrical power-line installers and repairers	0.8
Electricians	1.4
Firefighters	4.2
First-line supervisors/managers of construction trades and extraction workers	3.6
Heavy vehicle and mobile equipment service technicians and mechanics	1.4
Helpers, construction trades	2.4
Highway maintenance workers	2.9
Industrial and refractory machinery mechanics	3.3
Millwrights	4.6
Operating engineers and other construction equipment operators	1.2
Pest control workers	1.7
Railroad conductors and yardmasters	5.3

SOURCE: U.S. Department of Labor, Bureau of Labor Statistics, *Current Employment Statistics: Employment and Earnings* (2011), annual averages, table 39.

equality of opportunity does not exist," asserts Andrea H. Beller of University of Illinois at Urbana-Champaign, implying that this is indeed the situation of women.[32] However, there is no evidence to support the claim that women are driven into occupations with lower pay and prestige. Critics cite the existence of numerous occupations where women represent fewer than 10 percent of the workers. But on closer examination of the specifics of those male-dominated occupations, it becomes clear that men are actually taking on dirty, menial, and dangerous jobs that are undesirable to many women. Table 1-2 lists a few of these occupations from which women are allegedly excluded.

TABLE 1-3

Percentage of Fatal Occupational Injuries by Selected Occupations, 2010

Occupations	Percentage of Fatal Occupational Injuries
Education and health services	0.9
Leisure and hospitality	2.2
Professional and business services	2.5
Construction and extraction	9.5
Transportation and warehousing	13.1
Agriculture, forestry, fishing, and hunting	26.8
Mining	19.8

SOURCE: U.S. Department of Labor, Bureau of Labor Statistics, *Preliminary National Census of Fatal Occupational Injuries in 2010* (2010).

The high wage rates of such occupations reflect the high risks involved. Occupations of structural iron and steel workers, roofers, extraction workers, crane operators, and mechanics all demand physical strength and have high risks of workplace fatality and injury, as table 1-3 shows. In contrast to construction, extraction, installation, or transportation occupations, where about 50 percent of all the workplace fatalities occur, the "pink ghetto" occupations in the health, personal services, and food preparation and serving sectors together account for less than 5 percent of workplace fatalities.

To hire people to work in dangerous and unpleasant conditions, employers must offer them better pay than they would receive doing other low-skilled jobs in the market. Any low-skilled worker would otherwise choose to be a janitor rather than a roofer, or a cashier rather than an extraction worker. Women may be overrepresented in low-paying, low-skilled jobs, but it is by choice that they are not switching to the higher-paying, low-skilled jobs. Thus it does not make sense to persist in arguing that there are still occupations where women are underrepresented relative to the numbers of women who attempt to enter that occupation and, moreover, that women are being *funneled* and *confined* to low-paying, low-prestige occupations.

As for medium- and high-skilled jobs, women have steadily been making inroads into traditionally male occupational areas. Table

TABLE 1-4

Women's Share of Employment in Selected Occupations, 1970, 1998, and 2010

Occupations	Women's Share of Employment		
	1970	1998	2010
Architect	4	18	25
Cleric	3	12	17
Computer systems analyst or scientist	14	27	27
Dentist	4	20	25
Dietician	92	86	92
Editor or Reporter	42	51	47
Engineer	2	11	13
Lawyer	5	29	32
Librarian	82	83	80
Operations or systems researcher or analyst	11	42	47
Pharmacist	12	44	48
Physician	10	27	31
Psychologist	39	62	67
Public relations specialist	27	66	59
Registered nurse	97	93	91
Social worker	63	68	80
Teacher			
Prekindergarten or kindergarten	98	98	97
Elementary school	84	84	82
Secondary school	50	57	57
College or university	29	42	46

SOURCES: Francine Blau and Marianne A. Ferber, *The Economics of Men, Women, and Work,* 2nd ed., (Englewood Cliffs, N.J.: Prentice-Hall, 1992), table 5.3; U.S. Department of Labor, Bureau of Labor Statistics, *Employment and Earnings* (January 1999), annual averages, table 11; U.S. Department of Labor, Bureau of Labor Statistics, *Employment and Earnings* (January 2011), annual averages, table 11.

1-4 shows this progress. The percentages of women lawyers, dentists, physicians, engineers, pharmacists, and college professors have all risen considerably between 1970 and 2009. Given women's higher levels of educational achievement today, we can expect these percentages to keep rising.

Nevertheless, an AAUW report insisted that women are still "overwhelmingly clustered in low-wage, low-skill fields," citing

FIGURE 1-12

Percentage Monthly Change in the Number of Jobs in Selected Sectors, December 2007–December 2010

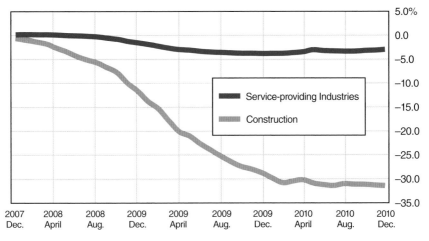

SOURCE: U.S. Department of Labor, Bureau of Labor Statistics, Establishment Survey.

findings that women comprise 87 percent of workers in the child-care industry and 86 percent in the health aide industry.[33] The AAUW claims that women are segregated into service sector jobs. But since the 2008-2009 recession, the so-called "ghetto" has actually been an oasis for women. For example, figure 1-12 graphs the monthly percentage change in the number of jobs changed in the service sector and the construction sector since the recession. The service sector, which makes up a large portion of the "pink ghetto," has lost approximately 3 percent of jobs since the start of the recession in December 2007, while the male-dominated construction sector has lost 31 percent of jobs.

From the beginning of the recession in December 2007 until December 2011, the unemployment rate for adult men grew from 4.5 percent to 8.0 percent, whereas for adult women it grew from 4.4 percent to 7.9 percent.[34] Thus, it is clear that women not only opt for jobs with more flexible schedules and less strenuous functions, but choose safer, more stable jobs in many cases. Men's higher wages are partly a compensation for risk-taking.

Women in Elective Office

Politics is another traditionally male arena where women have been increasingly active and successful. "More women than ever will serve in both houses of Congress, even though the numbers of candidates were not all-time highs," commented Debbie Walsh of the Center for American Women and Politics (CAWP) in 2010.[35] A record number of women won races in 2010 to serve in the 112th

TABLE 1-5

Summary of Women Candidates for U.S. Congress, 1970-2010

Election Year	Senate	House
1970	1 (0D, 1R)	25 (15D, 10R)
1972	2 (0D, 2R)	32 (24D, 8R)
1974	3 (2D, 1R)	44 (30D, 14R)
1976	1 (1D, 0R)	54 (34D, 20R)
1978	2 (1D, 1R)	46 (27D, 19R)
1980	5 (2D, 3R)	52 (27D, 25R)
1982	3 (1D, 2R)	55 (27D, 28R)
1984	10 (6D, 4R)	65 (30D, 35R)
1986	6 (3D, 3R)	64 (30D, 34R)
1988	2 (0D, 2R)	59 (33D, 26R)
1990	8 (2D, 6R)	69 (39D, 30R)
1992	11 (10D, 1R)	106 (70D, 36R)
1994	9 (4D, 5R)	112 (72D, 40R)
1996	9 (5D, 4R)	120 (77D, 42R)
1998	10 (7D, 3R)	121 (75D, 46R)
2000	6 (4D, 2R)	122 (80D, 42R)
2002	11 (8D, 3R)	124 (78D, 46R)
2004	10 (9D, 1R)	141 (88D, 53R)
2006	12 (8D, 4R)	136 (94D, 42R)
2008	7 (4D, 3R)	132 (95D, 37R)
2010	15 (9D, 6R)	138 (91D, 47R)

NOTE: Data since 1990 do not include the delegates from Washington, D.C., and the five territories.

SOURCE: Center for American Women and Politics, Eagleton Institute of Politics, Rutgers University, *National Information Bank on Women in Public Office*, 2011.

TABLE 1-6

Summary of Women Candidates for State Executive and Legislative Offices, 1974–2010

Election Year	Governor	Lt. Governor	Secretary of State	State Auditor	State Treasurer	State Legislator
1974	3 (1D, 2R)	4 (1D, 3R)	14 (6D, 8R)	5 (3D, 2R)	10 (8D, 2R)	1,125
1976	2 (2D, 0R)	1 (0D, 1R)	3 (0D, 3R)	0	6 (3D, 3R)	1,258
1978	1 (1D, 0R)	9 (6D, 3R)	16 (9D, 7R)	2 (2D, 0R)	10 (6D, 4R)	1,348
1980	0	3 (2D, 1R)	4 (1D, 3R)	3 (2D, 1R)	3 (2D, 1R)	1,426
1982	2 (2D, 0R)	7 (4D, 3R)	14 (7D, 7R)	1 (1D, 0R)	10 (6D, 4R)	1,643
1984	1 (1D, 0R)	6 (4D, 2R)	6 (4D, 2R)	4 (2D, 2R)	1 (1D, 0R)	1,756
1986	8 (3D, 5R)	11 (6D, 5R)	21 (14D, 7R)	6 (4D, 2R)	11 (7D, 4R)	1,813
1988	2 (2D, 0R)	2 (1D, 1R)	3 (2D, 1R)	2 (0D, 2R)	2 (1D, 1R)	1,853
1990	8 (4D, 4R)	19 (8D, 10R, 1Ind)	17 (8D, 9R)	7 (5D, 2R)	16 (8D, 8R)	2,064
1992	3 (2D, 1R)	7 (3D, 4R)	5 (3D, 2R)	1 (0D, 1R)	5 (3D, 2R)	2,375
1994	10 (6D, 3R, 1Ind)	29 (14D, 13R, 2Ind)	20 (8D, 12R)	4 (1D, 3R)	16 (11D, 5R)	2,285
1996	6 (3D, 3R)	9 (5D, 4R)	4 (4D, 0R)	2 (2D, 0R)	7 (3D, 4R)	2,274
1998	10 (6D, 4R)	25 (13D, 12R)	24 (14D, 10R)	8 (4D, 4R)	12 (7D, 5R)	2,280
2000	5 (3D, 2R)	5 (3D, 2R)	4 (2D, 2R)	4 (2D, 2R)	5 (3D, 2R)	2,228
2002	10 (9D, 1R)	21 (9D, 11R, 1IP)	13 (6D, 7R)	12 (6D, 6R)	12 (7D, 5R)	2,350
2004	3 (3D, 0R)	7 (6D, 1R)	7 (4D, 3R)	2 (1D, 1R)	4 (1D, 3R)	2,220
2006	10 (5D, 5R)	18 (12D, 6R)	21 (12D, 9R)	11 (6D, 5R)	14 (8D, 6R)	2,429
2008	4 (4D, 0R)	3 (1D, 2R)	6 (6D, 0R)	3 (3D, 0R)	2 (1D, 1R)	2,328
2010	10 (5D, 5R)	26 (16D, 10R)	12 (8D, 4R)	8 (4D, 4R)	9 (7D, 2R)	2,536

NOTE: Minor party candidates are included only if their parties have recently won statewide offices.

SOURCE: Center for American Women and Politics, Eagleton Institute of Politics, Rutgers University, *National Information Bank on Women in Public Office*, 2011.

Congress: 15 of them in the U.S. Senate and 138 women in the U.S. House of Representatives.

Tables 1-5 and 1-6 show how numbers of female candidates running for national and statewide offices have steadily increased. The number of candidates running for the U.S. House of Representatives is particularly remarkable, with 138 female candidates in 2010, a 13 percent increase over a decade ago and double the number of candidates only two decades earlier in 1990.

TABLE 1-7

Summary of Women in Congress

Congress	Dates	Women in Senate	Women in House	Total Women
92nd	1971–1973	2 (1D, 1R)	13 (10D, 3R)	15 (11D, 4R)
93rd	1973–1975	0	16 (14D, 2R)	16 (14D, 2R)
94th	1975–1977	0	19 (14D, 5R)	19 (14D, 5R)
95th	1977–1979	2 (2D, 0R)	18 (13D, 5R)	20 (15D, 5R)
96th	1979–1981	1 (0D, 1R)	16 (11D, 5R)	17 (11D, 6R)
97th	1981–1983	2 (0D, 2R)	21 (11D, 10R)	23 (11D, 12R)
98th	1983–1985	2 (0D, 2R)	22 (13D, 9R)	24 (13D, 11R)
99th	1985–1987	2 (0D, 2R)	23 (12D, 11R)	25 (12D, 13R)
100th	1987–1989	2 (1D, 1R)	23 (12D, 11R)	25 (13D, 12R)
101st	1989–1991	2 (1D, 1R)	29 (16D, 13R)	31 (17D, 14R)
102nd	1991–1993	4 (3D, 1R)	28 (19D, 9R)	32 (22D, 10R)
103rd	1993–1995	7 (5D, 2R)	47 (35D, 12R)	54 (40D, 14R)
104th	1995–1997	9 (5D, 4R)	48 (31D, 17R)	57 (36D, 21R)
105th	1997–1999	9 (6D, 3R)	54 (37D, 17R)	63 (43D, 20R)
106th	1999–2001	9 (6D, 3R)	56 (39D, 17R)	65 (45D, 20R)
107th	2001–2003	13 (9D, 4R)	59 (41D, 18R)	73 (51D, 22R)
108th	2003–2005	14 (9D, 5R)	60 (39D, 21R)	74 (48D, 26R)
109th	2005–2007	14 (9D, 5R)	68 (43D, 25R)	82 (52D, 30R)
110th	2007–2009	16 (11D, 5R)	72 (52D, 20R)	88 (63D, 25R)
111th	2009–2011	17 (13D, 4R)	73 (56D, 17R)	90 (69D, 21R)
112th	2011–2013	17 (12D, 5R)	71 (47D, 24R)	88 (59D, 29R)

SOURCE: Center for American Women and Politics, Eagleton Institute of Politics, Rutgers University, *National Information Bank on Women in Public Office*, 2011.

Table 1-7 lists the number of women from the two major political parties in Congress. Between 2001 and 2011, the total number of women in Congress increased from 73 to 88, a 20 percent increase. Consistent with these statistics are the results of a study by Jody Newman of the National Women's Political Caucus, which stated that there is a negligible difference between men and women's success rates in winning state and national elections.[36] She concluded that "women candidates *can* win…when they run." This is important to note since

FIGURE 1-13

Women in State Legislative Elections, 1992–2010

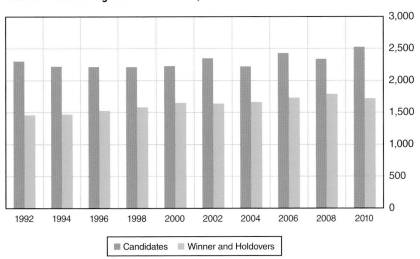

SOURCE: Center for American Women and Politics, Eagleton Institute of Politics, Rutgers University, *National Information Bank on Women in Public Office*, 2011.

FIGURE 1-14

Number of Women Candidates for U.S. Congressional Offices, 1970–2010

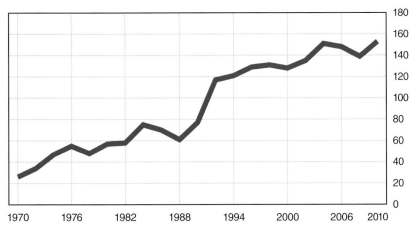

NOTES: Minor party candidates are included only if their parties have recently won statewide offices. Data since 1990 do not include the delegates from Washington, D.C., and the five territories.

SOURCE: Center for American Women and Politics, Eagleton Institute of Politics, Rutgers University, *National Information Bank on Women in Public Office*, 2011.

FIGURE 1-15

Number of Women in the U.S. Congress, 1971–2011

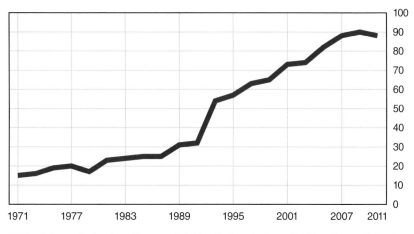

SOURCE: Center for American Women and Politics, Eagleton Institute of Politics, Rutgers University, *National Information Bank on Women in Public Office*, 2011.

there are many claims asserting that sex discrimination is the reason why women are underrepresented in politics.

Figure 1-13 displays a comparison of the number of women who ran for state legislative elections and the number who won, between 1992 and 2010. The trend for the number of female candidates to come closer to the number of female winners shows that not only are more women running for office, but more women are winning. Similarly, figures 1-14 and 1-15 show that although there were only 153 women candidates in U.S. congressional offices in 2011, 88 of them won elections. The success rate for women was thus almost 58 percent.

Voting Patterns

There are two differences between women and men as voters: the rates at which they vote, and the candidates whom women and men favor. Women have been voting at steadily increasing rates for decades, finally matching the male voting rate in the 1980 elections. Since then, women have been voting at greater rates than men, especially

TABLE 1-8

Differences in Voter Turnout for Presidential Elections by Sex, 1964–2008

Election Year	% Voting Age Population Who Reported Voting		Number Who Reported Voting (millions)	
	Women	Men	Women	Men
1964	67.0	71.9	39.2	37.5
1968	66.0	69.8	41.0	38.0
1972	62.0	64.1	44.9	40.9
1976	58.8	59.6	45.6	41.1
1980	59.4	59.1	49.3	43.8
1984	60.8	59.0	54.5	47.4
1988	58.3	56.4	54.5	47.7
1992	62.3	60.2	60.6	53.3
1996	55.5	52.8	56.1	48.9
2000	56.2	53.1	59.3	51.5
2004	60.1	56.3	67.3	58.5
2008	60.4	55.7	70.4	60.7

SOURCE: Center for American Women and Politics, Eagleton Institute of Politics, Rutgers University, *National Information Bank on Women in Public Office.*

in national elections. Since women account for the larger portion of adult Americans, greater absolute numbers of women than men have been voting in U.S. elections at least since 1964. Tables 1-8 and 1-9 present the differences between the percentage of eligible men and women voting and the absolute numbers of men and women who voted in presidential and nonpresidential elections.

Women and men tend to favor different candidates. Women collectively vote in greater numbers for Democratic candidates than for Republicans. This phenomenon is called the gender gap in voting, and is measured by the difference between the percentage of women and men voting for a given candidate, generally the candidate who wins. The gender gap in voting has been persistent in every presidential election since 1980. Ronald Reagan was elected in 1980 with 46 percent of female votes and 54 percent of male votes, making the gap 8 percent. The gender gap was pronounced in Bill Clinton's re-election in 1996,

TABLE 1-9

Differences in Voter Turnout for Nonpresidential Elections by Sex, 1966–2006

Election Year	% Voting Age Population Who Reported Voting		Number Who Reported Voting (millions)	
	Women	Men	Women	Men
1966	53.0	58.2	31.8	30.7
1970	52.7	56.8	33.8	32.0
1974	43.4	46.2	32.5	30.7
1978	45.3	46.6	36.3	33.3
1982	48.4	48.7	42.3	38.0
1986	46.1	45.8	42.2	37.7
1990	45.4	44.6	43.3	38.7
1994	45.3	44.7	45.0	40.7
1998	42.4	41.4	43.7	39.4
2002	43.0	41.4	47.1	41.8
2006	44.7	42.4	51.0	45.1

SOURCE: Center for American Women and Politics, Eagleton Institute of Politics, Rutgers University, *National Information Bank on Women in Public Office.*

when he received 54 percent of women's votes and only 43 percent of men's votes, making the gender gap 11 percent.[37]

The gender gap in voting was evidenced in the 2008 elections. In the 2008 presidential election, 56 percent of women voted for the Democratic candidate, Barack Obama, while 43 percent of women voted for the Republican candidate, John McCain. In comparison, men voted evenly among the presidential candidates, with 49 percent voting for the Democratic candidate and 48 percent voting for the Republican candidate.[38] Since 56 percent of women while only 49 percent of men voted for the winner, Barack Obama, the gender gap in voting was 7 percent.

NOTES

1. Qingyan Shang and Bruce Weinberg, *Opting for Families: Recent Trends in the Fertility of Highly Educated Women* (Working Paper No. 15074, National Bureau of Economics Research, 2009).

2. Deborah Rhode, *Speaking of Sex: The Denial of Gender Inequality* (Cambridge, Massachusetts: Harvard University Press, 1997), 142.

3. John Robinson and Geoffrey Godbey, *Time for Life: The Surprising Ways Americans Use their Time*, (University Park, Pennsylvania: Pennsylvania State University Press, 1997).

4. David Autor and David Dorn, *Inequality and Specialization: The Growth of Low-Skill Service Jobs in the United States* (Working Paper No. 15150, National Bureau for Economic Research, 2009); and Patricia Cortes and Jose Tessada, *Cheap Maids and Nannies: How Low-Skilled Immigration is Changing the Labor Supply of High-Skilled American Women,* (working paper, 2008).

5. U.S. Department of Labor, Bureau of Labor Statistics, *Women in the Labor Force: A Databook*, Report 1018 (Washington, D.C., 2009).

6. U.S. Census Bureau, *Men's and Women's Earnings by State, 2009 American Community Survey* (Washington, D.C., 2010).

7. U.S. Department of Labor, Bureau of Labor Statistics, "Median usual weekly earnings of wage and salary workers by hours usually worked and sex, 2010 annual averages – continued," in *Highlights of Women's Earnings in 2007* (Washington, D.C., 2011), 41. Statistic refers to workers who usually work exactly 40 hours a week.

8. CONSAD, *An Analysis of Reasons for the Disparity in Wages Between Men and Women* (Pittsburg, 2009). Prepared for the U.S. Department of Labor.

9. Jody Feder and Linda Levine, *Pay Equity Legislation in the 110th Congress*, CRS *Report for Congress RL31867* (Washington, DC: Congressional Research Service, Updated 5 January 2007).

10. Randy Albelda, *Equal Pay for Equal Work? New Evidence on the Persistence of the Gender Pay Gap*, Statement at the House of Representatives, Joint Economic Committee, April 28, 2009.

11. Commission of the European Communities, *Tackling the pay gap between women and men* (Brussels, 2007); Mary Cornish, "Closing the Global Gender Pay Gap: Securing Justice for Women's Work," *Comparative Labor Law and Policy Journal* (2007) 28: 219; International Confederation of Free Trade Unions. *Trade Union World Briefing. Equality through pay equity* (Brussels, 2003), 1; International Labour Organization, *Breaking through the Glass Ceiling—Women in Management* (Geneva,

updated 2004); International Labour Organization, *Global Employment Trends for Women* (Geneva, 2009), 32; Evelyn Murphy, *Getting Even: Why Women Don't Get Paid Like Men—and What to Do About It* (New York: Touchstone, 2005), 267; World Economic Forum, *Global Gender Gap Report* (Geneva, 2007), Preface, vii.

12. A quantitative analysis of studies that reported sex discrimination conducted by Henry Tosi of University of Florida and engineer Steven W. Einbender of Electronic Data Systems found that of the eleven studies showing discrimination, ten used fewer than four explanatory variables. On the other hand, only three out of the ten studies that did not report discrimination used fewer than four explanatory variables. See Tosi and Einbender, "The Effects of the Type and Amount of Information in Sex Discrimination Research: A Meta-Analyis," *The Academy of Management Journal* 28, no. 3 (1985): 712–23.

13. June O'Neill, "The Gender Gap in Wages, Circa 2000," *American Economic Review* 93, no. 2 (2003): 309–14.

14. Paula England, "Gender Inequality in Labor Markets: The Role of Motherhood and Segregation," *Social Politics: International Studies in Gender, State and Society* 12, no. 2 (2005): 264–88; Lalith Munasinghe, Alice Henriques, and Tania Reif, "The Gender Gap in Wage Returns on Job Tenure and Experience," *Labour Economics* 15, no. 6 (2008): 1296–316; June O'Neill and Dave M. O'Neill, "What do Wage Differentials tell us about Labor Market Discrimination?" (Working Paper No. 11240, National Bureau for Economic Research, 2005); Jane Waldfogel, "Working Mothers Then and Now: A Cross-Cohort Analysis of the Effects of Maternity Leave on Women's Pay," *Gender and Family Issues in the Workplace*, ed. Francine D. Blau and Ronald G. Ehrenberg (New York: Russell Sage Foundation, 1997); and Jane Waldfogel, *What Children Need* (Cambridge: Harvard University Press, 2006).

15. Marianne Bertrand and Kevin Hallock, "The Gender Gap in Top Corporate Jobs," *Industrial and Labor Relations Review* 55, no. 1 (2001): 3–21.

16. Helen Levy, "Health Insurance and the Wage Gap" (Working Paper No. 11975, National Bureau for Economic Research, 2006).

17. Rachel Croson and Uri Gneezy, "Gender Differences in Preferences," *Journal of Economic Literature* 47, no. 2 (2009): 448–74.

18. Linda Babcock and Sara Laschever, *Women Don't Ask* (Princeton: Princeton University Press, 2003); Lisa Baron, "Ask and you shall receive: Gender differences in negotiators' beliefs about requests for a higher salary," *Human Relations* 56 (2003): 635–62; Rachel Croson and Uri Gneezy, "Gender Differences in Preferences," *Journal of Economic Literature* 47, no.2 (2009): 448–74; and Deborah A. Small et al, "Gender and the initiation of negotiations in ambiguous situations," (mimeo, Carnegie Mellon University, 2003).

19. U.S. Government Accountability Office, *Women's Pay: Converging Characteristics of Men and Women in the Federal Workforce Help Explain the Narrowing Pay Gap*, 2009.

20. Jane Waldfogel, "Working Mothers Then and Now: A Cross-Cohort Analysis of the Effects of Maternity Leave on Women's Pay," in *Gender and Family Issues in the Workplace*, edited by Francine D. Blair and Ronald G. Ehrenberg (New York: Russell Sage Foundation, 1989), 92–126.

21. Judy Goldberg Dey and Catherine Hill, *Behind the Pay Gap*, American Association of University Women Educational Foundation (Washington, D.C.: American Association of University Women Educational Foundation, 2007).

22. Elizabeth Fox-Genovese, *Feminism is Not the Story of My Life* (New York: Doubleday, 1996).

23. Marianne Bertrand, Claudia Goldin, and Lawrence F. Katz, Dynamics of the Gender Gap for Young Professionals in the Corporate and Financial Sectors (Working Paper No. 14681, National Bureau of Economic Research, 2009).

24. Dey and Hill, *Behind the Pay Gap*.

25. U.S. Government Accountability Office, *Women's Pay: Converging Characteristics of Men and Women in the Federal Workforce Help Explain the Narrowing Pay Gap*, 2009.

26. Fair Pay Act of 2011. 1st Session S.788: 112th Congress, April 12, 2011.

27. Carol Hymowitz and Timothy D. Schellhardt, "The Corporate Woman (A Special Report): The Glass Ceiling: Why Women Can't Seem to Break the Invisible Barrier That Blocks Them From the Top Jobs," *Wall Street Journal*, March 24, 1986.

28. Glass Ceiling Commission, *Good for Business: Making Full Use of the Nation's Human Capital* (Washington, D.C.: U.S. Department of Labor, 1995), 25.

29. Ibid.

30. Korn/Ferry Institute, *34th Annual Board of Directors Study* (Los Angeles, California: Korn/Ferry Institute, 2008), http://www.kornferry.com/Publication/9955; Korn/Ferry International, KFMC100 Board Leadership at America's Most Valuable Public Companies, (Los Angeles, California: Korn/Ferry Institute, 2011), http://www.kornferryinstitute.com/files/pdf1/KFMC100.pdf.

31. U.S. Government Accountability Office, *Women in Management: Analysis of Selected Data from the Current Population Survey* (Congressional Briefing Slides, 2001).

32. Andrea H. Beller, "Occupational Segregation by Sex: Determinants and Changes," *Journal of Human Resources* 17 (1982): 371–92.

33. American Association of University Women, *Pay Equity and Workplace Opportunity: A Simple Matter of Fairness*, 2011: 2, http://www.aauw.org/act/issue_advocacy/actionpages/upload/PayEquity_12.pdf (accessed October 2, 2011).

34. U.S. Department of Labor, Bureau of Labor Statistics, 2007–2011.

35. Center for the American Women and Politics, "Record Number of Women to Serve in Senate and House," news release, November 5, 2008.

36. Jody Newman, "The Gender Story: Women as Voters and Candidates in the 1996 Elections," *America at the Polls 1996*, eds. Regina Dougherty, Evett C. Ladd, David Wilber, and Lynn Zayachkiwsky (Storrs, Conn.: Roper Center for Public Opinion Research, 1997), 106.

37. Center for American Women and Politics, "The Gender Gap" (New Brunswick, 2008), http://www.cawp.rutgers.edu/fast_facts/voters/documents/GGPresVote.pdf.

38. Women's Vote Watch, "Gender Gap Evident in the 2008 Election: Women, Unlike Men, Show Clear Preference for Obama over McCain," news release, November 5, 2008, http://www.cawp.rutgers.edu/press_room/news/documents/Press Release_11-05-08_womensvote.pdf.

PART
II

Reaching the Top: Women's Educational Attainment

*T*he narrowing gender gap in career success and compensation has occurred, in large part, because of the strides women have made in educational attainment. Women are the majority of college and university students and receive well over half of bachelor's and master's degrees as well as half of doctoral degrees awarded in the United States. This chapter analyzes women's educational attainment and success.

Educational Attainment

Figure 2-1 shows the percentage of higher education degrees earned by women from 1970 through 2010. In 2009, over 57 percent of bachelor's degrees were awarded to women. The same year, three women earned an associate's or master's degree for every two men who earned one of those degrees, and as many women as men earned doctoral degrees. This progress in education is remarkable, given that in 1970 women only earned 43 percent of associate's and bachelor's degrees, 40 percent of master's degrees, 5 percent of first professional degrees, and 13 percent of doctoral degrees.

Educational Choices

Women not only have made considerable gains in educational attainment, but are increasingly entering into previously male-dominated educational programs. Traditionally, women and men

FIGURE 2-1

Share of Degrees Earned by Women, 1970–2020

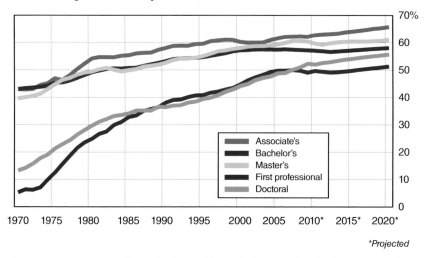

*Projected

SOURCE: U.S. Department of Education, National Center for Education Statistics, *Digest of Education Statistics 2009* (2010).

enrolled in different educational programs. To some extent this remains true today. For example, the majority of bachelor's degrees in library sciences, consumer services, human services, communications, and humanities were conferred on women in 2009, whereas degrees in mathematically oriented fields such as engineering and computer science were conferred on men. Figure 2-2 shows that only 16 percent of bachelor's degrees in engineering and engineering technologies and only 18 percent of degrees in the computer and information science sector were earned by women in the 2008–2009 academic year.[1]

While women remain underrepresented in the engineering and computer science degree programs, more women have earned degrees in the fields previously dominated by men, such as business, medicine, and the law. In 2009, women earned 73 percent of bachelor's degrees in legal studies and 85 percent of bachelor's degrees in health-related areas of study. The percentage of degrees awarded to women in business, law, dentistry, and medicine has significantly increased since 1970, as depicted in figures 2-3 through 2-6. In 1970, women earned fewer than 10 percent of degrees in these fields, but

FIGURE 2-2

Share of Bachelor's Degrees Awarded to Women, by Field of Study, 2008–2009

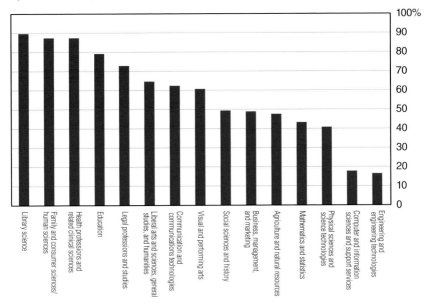

SOURCE: U.S. Department of Education, National Center for Education Statistics, *Digest of Education Statistics 2009* (2010) Table 286.

FIGURE 2-3

Share of Master's Degrees in Business Awarded to Women, 1970–2009

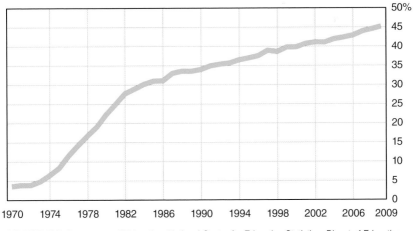

SOURCE: U.S. Department of Education, National Center for Education Statistics, *Digest of Education Statistics, 2009* (2010).

FIGURE 2-4

Share of Law Degrees Awarded to Women, 1970–2009

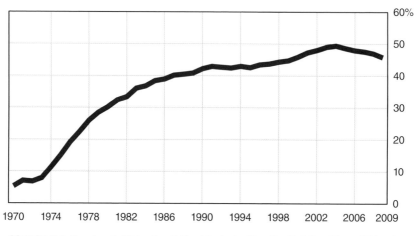

SOURCE: U.S. Department of Education, National Center for Education Statistics, *Digest of Education Statistics 2009* (2010).

FIGURE 2-5

Share of Dentistry Degrees Awarded to Women, 1970–2009

SOURCE: U.S. Department of Education, National Center for Education Statistics, *Digest of Education Statistics 2009* (2010).

today women earn approximately 50 percent of medical and law degrees and 45 percent of business and dentistry degrees. In less than a half a century, women have striven for their place in traditionally male-dominated fields and have shown exceptional staying power.

FIGURE 2-6

Share of Medical Degrees Awarded to Women, 1970–2009

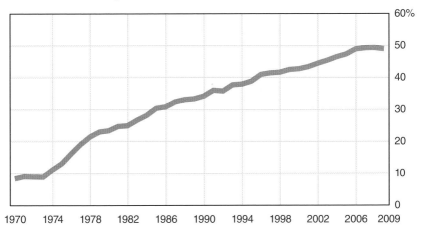

SOURCE: U.S. Department of Education, National Center for Education Statistics, *Digest of Education Statistics 2009* (2010).

Extending Title IX

Despite this progress, the U.S. Department of Education is weighing whether to extend Title IX, now used to enforce equal participation by men and women in college sports, to math and science. Title IX, a 1972 amendment to the 1964 Civil Rights Act, was intended to ensure that women would not be discriminated against in any educational program or activity receiving federal funding.[2] In 1979, the Department of Education interpreted Title IX to mean that all universities receiving federal funding must satisfy at least one requirement of a three-prong test in order to be in compliance with Title IX. This test, which applies to intercollegiate athletic programs, requires that universities receiving federal funding either (1) ensure that participation in intercollegiate athletic programs by gender is proportionate to undergraduate enrollment by gender, (2) have a continuing tradition of expanding intercollegiate athletic programs for the underrepresented gender, or (3) fully accommodate the athletic interests and abilities of the underrepresented gender.[3]

Over the years, however, court rulings have placed strong emphasis on the proportionality requirement, and complying with this requirement has become the only sure way for universities to protect themselves against Title IX lawsuits.[4] This trend was enforced in April 2010, when the Department of Education ruled that colleges could not use surveys to show that women did not want to participate in sports. So, to be safe, colleges follow the proportionality requirement. If 60 percent of a college's students are women, then 60 percent of the varsity sports slots must go to women. To satisfy the courts, Title IX has led universities around the country to eliminate a number of men's teams (such as men's gymnastics) and deprive many male athletes of the opportunity to compete.[5]

Title IX, with its emphasis on proportionality, fails to take into consideration that men have demonstrated greater interest in participating in sports than women. Even at women's colleges participation is low despite the large female populations. For example, at Smith College, Mount Holyoke, and Wellesley College only 10, 11, and 12 percent of students respectively participate in varsity sports. This divergence in interests between men and women is a problem for the application of Title IX not only in college sports but in academics.

In recent years, there has been a significant movement to extend stricter enforcement of Title IX to academic programs. In particular, there has been a recent push within the Obama administration to apply Title IX to science, technology, engineering, and mathematics (STEM) education programs, academic areas where women have historically been underrepresented.[6] This has been a particular concern of the White House Council on Women and Girls, which includes all Cabinet secretaries as members and is headed by Assistant to the President and Senior Advisor Valerie Jarrett. The Council's mission is to "to enhance, support and coordinate the efforts of existing programs for women and girls."

At a June 23, 2009 White House conference held on the thirty-seventh anniversary of Title IX, government officials discussed a proposal endorsed by Ms. Jarrett and Ms. Russlynn Ali, Assistant Secretary for Civil Rights, to extend the Title IX proportionality requirement to selection of courses and major academic subjects at universities.[7] Although the proposal was rejected and the Obama administration opted not to enact a proportionality requirement in these fields, the administration did decide to use "somewhat new enforcement" to ensure that girls and women are not counseled against choosing STEM courses and majors.[8] The administration also reserved the right to expand Title IX yet further to achieve gender parity in these fields.

Exactly one year later, on June 23, 2010, White House Senior Policy Analyst of Science and Technology Policy Jessie DeAro made a statement declaring the administration's continuing support for the extension of Title IX to academics.[9] DeAro praised the federal Title IX Interagency Working Group, coordinated by the Department of Justice and consisting of representatives from the National Aeronautics and Space Administration, the National Science Foundation, the Department of Energy, and the Department of Education, for working to promote equity in STEM programs at American universities.[10] The administration has decided currently only to monitor discrimination in STEM academic programs, especially in terms of academic and career counseling. However, as more emphasis is placed on Title IX compliance in STEM education programs, the administration might implement an academic proportionality requirement similar to the one that applies to intercollegiate athletics.

Extending Title IX to academics is a highly flawed policy even if the extension is restricted to counseling and course and major selection. There is no evidence of discrimination against women in STEM courses, majors, and careers. As discussed above, women have been able to enter previously male-dominated fields. While it is true that women still remain underrepresented in fields such as science, math, engineering, and technology, there is no reason to believe that this is due to discrimination. Although women represented only 11 percent of tenure-track job applicants in electrical engineering and 12 percent of applicants in physics, they received 32 percent and 20 percent of the job offers in these fields, respectively,[11] which strongly suggests that STEM programs not only do not discriminate against women but actively recruit them.

It is more likely that women simply choose not to enter these fields despite efforts encouraging them to do so. And if gender discrimination is not an issue, it is unwise to try to increase artificially the number of women in these fields through Title IX quotas.

Course- and major-selection counseling should take into consideration interest and aptitude, regardless of gender. If the administration insists on extending Title IX to academic programs, universities will fear discrimination lawsuits unless they can show gender parity in STEM courses and academic programs. This could result in the adoption of an official or de facto proportionality requirement.

Such a requirement would harm students, because math, science, and engineering programs would be forced to choose more students from a smaller female pool and fewer students from a larger male pool. As a result, less qualified female students would do poorly in math and science classes, while more qualified male students would be denied the opportunity to take these classes. Title IX would then only penalize male students while failing to benefit female students. Moreover, America would suffer the penalty over the next generation of having a smaller cohort of truly gifted young scientists trained to meet the challenges of the coming decades.

NOTES

1. U.S. Department of Education, National Center for Education Statistics, Institute of Education Sciences, *Digest of Education Statistics 2009* (Washington, D.C.: U.S. Department of Education, 2010) Table 286. http://nces.ed.gov/programs/digest/d10/tables/dt10_286.asp (accessed: September 6, 2011).

2. U.S. Department of Education, Office for Civil Rights, *Further Clarification of Intercollegiate Athletics Policy Guidance Regarding Title IX Compliance*, issued July 11, 2003, http://www2.ed.gov/about/offices/list/ocr/title9guidance Final.html.

3. Ibid.

4. Eric Pearson, *National Review: Benching The Title IX Changes*, News story, National Public Radio, June 1, 2010, http://www.npr.org/templates/story/story.php?storyId=127306783.

5. Ibid.

6. Jessie DeAro, "Bringing Title IX to Classrooms and Labs," The White House Council on Women and Girls blog, June 24, 2010, http://www.whitehouse.gov/blog/2010/06/24/bringing-title-ix-classrooms-and-labs.

7.   Diana Furchtgott-Roth, "Obama, Title IX, and Academics?" RealClearMarkets, blog, July 9, 2009,

8.   Ibid.

9.   DeAro, "Bringing Title IX to Classrooms and Labs."

10. Ibid.

11. Committee on Gender Differences in the Careers of Science, Engineering, and Mathematics Faculty; Committee on Women in Science, Engineering, and Medicine; National Research Council, *Gender Differences at Critical Transitions in the Careers of Science, Engineering and Mathematics Faculty*, National Academy of Sciences (Washington, D.C: The National Academies Press, 2009), 36.

PART III

The Marriage Penalty, Social Security Disincentives, and Other Ways Government Programs Increase Poverty among Women

*W*omen have closed the gender gap in wages and now exceed men in educational attainment. Nevertheless, rates of poverty among women are higher today than they were in 1970 and have increased steadily over the last decade. Why should women at the bottom of the economic ladder fare so badly even as other women mount higher on the economic ladder? To address this question, it is necessary to understand why more women than men fall into poverty and how the perverse incentives created by government programs increase the prospects that women will find themselves in poverty.

The Feminization of Poverty

The term "feminization of poverty" was coined to describe the higher incidence of female poverty. Although women constituted 51 percent of the population in 2010,[1] they accounted for 55 percent of all people

FIGURE 3-1

Share of Population below the Poverty Line by Sex, 1970–2010

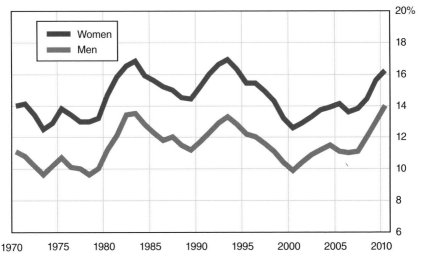

SOURCE: U.S. Bureau of the Census, Current Population Survey, Annual Social and Economic Supplements.

living in poverty. As figure 3-1 illustrates, between 1970 and 2010, female poverty rates consistently exceeded male poverty rates by approximately three percentage points.[2] In 2010, 16 percent of women, compared to 14 percent of men, were in poverty.[3]

Census data show how rates of poverty vary over the life cycle. While poverty rates for boys and girls are almost equal, poverty rates for men and women diverge early in adulthood and differ significantly throughout adulthood, as is shown in figure 3-2. In 2010, 25 percent of women between the ages of 18 and 24 were in poverty, compared to only 19 percent of men in that age range. Over the age of 65, women are 1.7 times as likely to be in poverty as men.

Important social trends explain the gap between male and female poverty rates. Two reasons are particularly important. First, there has been a trend of young women heading one-person households. Women are postponing marriage, creating a large number of young single women. Prior to 1973, the median age at first marriage for women was below 21 years of age. Since 1973, as shown in figure 3-3, the median age at first marriage for women has steadily risen to

FIGURE 3-2

Poverty Rate by Age and Sex, 2010

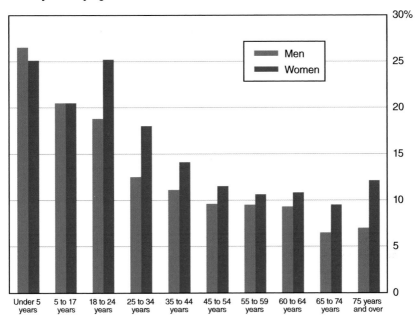

SOURCE: U.S. Bureau of the Census, Current Population Survey, Annual Social and Economic Supplement.

FIGURE 3-3

Median Age at First Marriage by Sex, 1970–2010

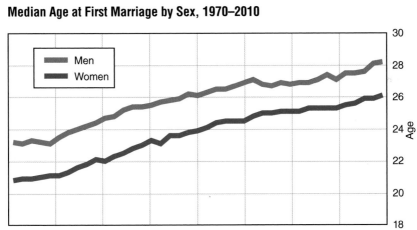

SOURCES: U.S. Census Bureau, *Current Population Reports*, series P20-514, "Marital Status and Living Arrangements: March 1998 (Update)," and earlier reports; Current Population Survey, *March and Annual Social and Economic Supplements*, 2008 and earlier.

FIGURE 3-4

Marital Status of Women, Percentage Distribution, 1971–2010

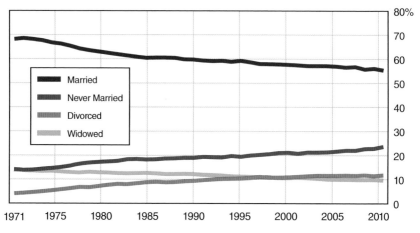

NOTE: Women ages 18 and older.

SOURCES: U.S. Census Bureau *Statistical Abstract*: 1971, no. 38; 1972, no. 46; 1980, no. 51; 1983, no. 44; 1989, no. 50; 1990, no. 50; 1991, no. 50; 1992, no. 49; 1993, no. 49; 1994, no. 59; 1995, no. 58; 1997, no. 58; 1998, no. 61; Historical Statistics, series A, pp. 160-71; U.S. Bureau of the Census, unpublished data; U.S. Census Bureau, 1970 Census of Population, vol. I, part 1, and Current Population Reports, P20-533, and earlier reports; and "Families and Living Arrangements"; http://www.census.gov/population/www/socdemo/hh-fam.html.

age 26 in 2010. This trend reflects the increasing number of women attending college and pursuing career opportunities upon graduation, as well as cultural factors.

Second, the rising incidence of divorce has contributed to the growing population of young single women. Figure 3-4 illustrates the distribution of American women, who are at least 18 years old, by marital status. In 1971, 14 percent of adult women were single and only 4 percent were divorced. By 2010, while the percentage of single women grew to 27 percent, the percentage of divorced women increased to 11 percent.

The postponement of marriage and the high incidence of divorce have both led to an increase in the relative population of young female-headed households, a substantial percentage of which are also susceptible to poverty. It is notable that 29 percent of female households without a husband are living in poverty. In contrast, only 5 percent of married couples and 14 percent of male households without a wife are poor.[4]

FIGURE 3-5

Share of All Births to Unmarried Women, by Race and Hispanic Origin, Selected Years,1960–2009

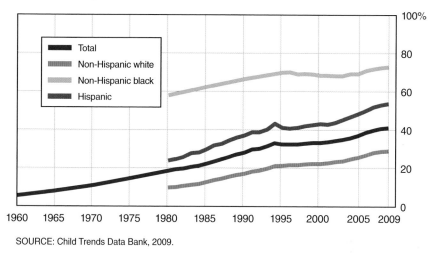

SOURCE: Child Trends Data Bank, 2009.

Many female-headed households have children present either from earlier marriages or from relationships outside of marriage. In such situations, women are more likely to be the custodial parent. In 2010, 79 percent of the custodial parents were mothers. Moreover, as shown in figure 3-5, the illegitimacy rate has increased significantly, from 10.7 percent of all births to unmarried women of childbearing age in 1970 to a peak of 41 percent of all births to unmarried women of childbearing age in 2009.

Even as the illegitimacy rate has climbed, the total birth rate has declined from about 88 births per 1,000 women of childbearing age in 1970 to 67 births per 1,000 women of childbearing age in 2009, as figure 3-6 shows. The combination of declining fertility and increased illegitimacy has led to an increase in the percentage of illegitimate births and the proportion of families headed by unmarried women. Figure 3-7 shows that the percentage of female head of households with children has more than doubled from 10 percent in 1970 to 23 percent in 2010.

Employment opportunities are more limited for parents who bear most of the responsibilities of raising children. Childrearing

FIGURE 3-6

Births per 1,000 Women Ages 15–44, 1970–2009

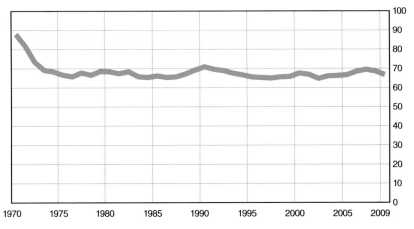

SOURCES: U.S. Census Bureau, *Historical Statistics*, vol. 1, series B28-35, p. 52; *Vital Statistics*: 1972, pp. 1-30; *Statistical Abstract*: 1980, no. 95; 1987, no. 86; 1990, no. 90; 1992, no. 89; 1994, no. 100; 1995, no. 94. *Monthly Vital Statistics Report*: 1997, vol. 45, no. 11(s), table 15; 1998, vol. 46, no. 11(s), table 17; *National Vital Statistics Report*: 1999, vol. 47, no. 25; 2000, vol. 48, no. 14; 2001, vol. 49, no. 5; 2002, vol. 51, no. 2; 2003, vol. 51, no. 11; 2005, vol. 54, no. 2; 2005, vol. 54, no. 8; 2007, vol. 56, no. 6; 2009, vol. 57, no. 7; 2009, vol. 57, no. 12; National Center for Health Statistics.

FIGURE 3-7

Percentage Distribution of Families with Children under 18 by Family Head, 1970–2010

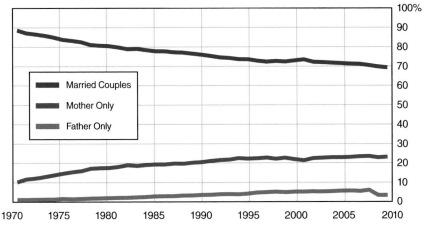

NOTE: Data for 1970 and 1980 include revisions from the Census Bureau.

SOURCE: U.S. Bureau of the Census, *Current Population Reports*, series P20-515, "Household and Family Characteristics: March 1998 (Update)," and earlier reports; U.S. Census Bureau, Current Population Survey, March and Annual Social and Economic Supplements, 2008 and earlier.

activities consume time that could otherwise be spent earning more income. Parents responsible for child-raising must often choose flexible working hours over higher-paid positions. In contrast, a family with two parents can have two earners, one of whom can accept a more highly compensated but inflexible position, while the other accepts a more variable-hour position.

In addition to being responsible for childcare, women are more likely to care for elderly or disabled family members. Some studies suggest that two-thirds of all unpaid caregivers are women.[5] Employment and earning opportunities for caregivers are limited because these women often work part-time or take leave from the workforce to care for a family member.

How Government Programs Increase Poverty among Women

Poverty-prone, unmarried, female-headed households are not entirely the result of demographic trends. Some government programs themselves influence the incidence of female-headed households and the poverty associated with them.

Public policy can affect individuals' choices and influence even the most intimate choices about whether or not to marry and how to provide for one's family. After the passage of the 1996 Personal Responsibility and Work Opportunity Reconciliation Act, which limited the period people could collect welfare and removed disincentives to work and to marry, the welfare rolls fell by 60 percent. Even the Great Recession did not undo this historic decline in the welfare rolls. After the worst of the recession in 2009, welfare rolls increased by only 15 percent.

However, when many of the provisions of the Patient Protection and Affordable Care Act take effect in 2014, unwed Americans may find it even more advantageous—financially, anyway—to stay single rather than to marry. And women, or possibly men who earn less than their wives, will face greater incentives to leave the workforce. These perverse incentives can only worsen women's economic circumstances in the long run.

These perverse incentives arise from the federal government's offer of tax credits to singles and families with incomes between 133 percent and 400 percent of the poverty line. These credits can be used only to buy health insurance through the new health exchanges. The size of the credits will be linked to the second-lowest cost plan in the area, and the credits are structured so that health insurance premium contributions are limited to percentages of income for specified income levels, as shown in table 3-1 below.

TABLE 3-1

Health Insurance Premium Tax Credits by Household Income

Household Income as Percent of Federal Poverty Line	Premium Payment as Percentage of Income
Up to 133%	2%
133%–150%	3% to 4%
150%–200%	4% to 6.3%
200%–250%	6.3% to 8.05%
250%–300%	8.05% to 9.5%
300%–400%	9.5%

SOURCE: U.S. Statutes, *Health Care and Education Reconciliation Act of 2010*, Section 1001(a)

The Medicare surtax affects singles earning $200,000 and couples earning $250,000, and increases the marriage penalty at upper-income levels. More important, at the low end of the income scale and into the middle class, the health insurance premium credits in the new law are linked to the poverty line, resulting in new and steep marriage penalties.

With $10,890 as the poverty line for one person and an additional $3,820 for a spouse, marriage in 2014 will mean less government help with health insurance premiums. Americans will receive credits for the purchase of health insurance for incomes up to 400 percent of the poverty line, now $43,560 for singles and $58,840 for a couple. Median household income was $49,445 in 2010, and 61 percent of all families, the majority, were at or below 400 percent of the poverty line. In such circumstances, marriage means health insurance will cost more, because two married individuals may exceed the income ceiling to get government help with health insurance premiums. If they stayed single, they might qualify.

Since premium credits shrink as income rises, making premiums more costly, there will exist an incentive to report less income. That would discourage marriage between two employed persons, or would encourage nonmarital cohabitation and children.

Two singles would each be able to earn $43,000 and still receive help to purchase health insurance, but if they got married and combined their earnings to $86,000, they would be far above the limit. As a married couple, the most they could earn and still get government help would be $58,000, a difference of almost $30,000, or 32 percent. This would be a substantial disincentive to getting married or to working while married.

The penalty extends also to single mothers. Say Sally is a single mother earning $43,130, putting her and her baby at 300 percent of the poverty line for a household of two. They would be eligible for the health insurance premium assistance credit.

But what if Sally wants to marry Sam, the father of her child, who earns $43,560, and is at 400 percent of the federal poverty line for a household of one? Their total earnings, at $87,690, would exceed the 400 percent of the poverty line for a family of three, $74,120. Married, they would no longer receive help with their health insurance premiums, despite both earning the credit when unmarried. In order to keep her government health insurance benefit, Sally could only marry someone earning less than $30,000.

As well as discouraging marriage, the health care law gives an incentive to the lower-earning spouse, generally the woman, to leave the labor force, lowering the returns to her education and damaging her future job prospects.

With over half of poor households headed by single mothers, our laws should encourage rather than discourage marriage. It is well known that avoidance of marriage among low-wage earners increases poverty rates, especially for women. Data from the Census Bureau show that in 2010, the latest year available, 51 percent of families below the poverty line were headed by single mothers. In

FIGURE 3-8

Life Expectancy at Birth by Sex, 1970–2010

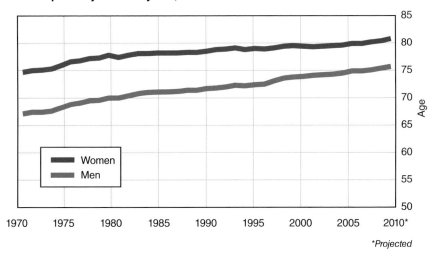

*Projected

SOURCES: U.S. Census Bureau, *Historical Statistics*, vol. 1, series B, pp. 107-15; *National Center for Health Statistics, Health, United States, 2008*, table 26, p. 203; *National Vital Statistics Report: 2009*, vol. 57, no. 14; 2009, vol. 58, no. 1; *Statistical Abstract*, 1998, no. 128; *Vital Statistics, 1985*, no. 102; *World Almanac, 1998*, p. 973.

the African American community, the rates were even more dramatic. Of all African American families at or below the poverty line, 74 percent were headed by single mothers. The structure of health premium credits in the new bill will further increase the number of fatherless families, leading to more poverty and a lower quality of life.

Women are more likely than men to experience poverty in old age. One reason for this is simply that women are now likely to live to an advanced age. People today are living longer, and women, in general, are living longer than men, as shown in figure 3-8.

In 1970, male life expectancy was 67 years, and female life expectancy was 75 years. By 2010, the projected life expectancy at birth for men had risen to 76 years and to 81 years for women. Women thus typically survive their husbands by several years both because of a greater life expectancy and because women tend to marry men older than themselves. As a result, retirement savings, which may have been adequate at the date of retirement, may dwindle in later years when the wife is more likely to be a single survivor.

This population is difficult to measure exactly. The elderly usually do not work, and so there may be elderly with low incomes that are well-off because they have substantial savings, while others with low incomes and low savings live meagerly. Income is easy to measure, while wealth and consumption are more challenging. Income itself does not reveal whether an elderly person can afford to live lavishly or poorly. The Pew Research Center found that in 2009, households headed by those 65 and over had 47 times the net wealth of younger ones (with heads below 35).[6]

Perversely, the Social Security system meant to sustain people in their old age can actually work against women, especially married working women. These women lose part of their contributions upon retirement, which works against women's interests and distorts their decisions in the labor market. Penalties are greatest for women who have invested the most in their education, hoping to shatter the glass ceiling and compete with men.

NOTES

1. U.S. Census Bureau, *Income, Poverty, and Health Insurance Coverage in the United States: 2010, Current Population Reports*, P60-236 (Washington, D.C.: U.S. Government Printing Office, 2011), http://www.census.gov/hhes/www/cpstables/032011/pov/new01_100_01.htm.

2. The Census Bureau defines poverty rate as the percentage of population below 100 percent of the poverty threshold. Figure 3-1 represents the share of each gender below 100 percent of the poverty line.

3. U.S. Census Bureau, *Income, Poverty, and Health Insurance Coverage in the United States: 2010, Current Population Reports*, P60-236 (Washington, D.C.: U.S. Government Printing Office, 2011), http://www.census.gov/hhes/www/cpstables/032011/pov/new01_100_01.htm.

4. Ibid.

5. Richard W. Johnson and Joshua M. Wiener, *A Profile of Frail Older Americans and Their Caregivers* (Washington, D.C: The Urban Institute: 2006), http://www.urban.org/publications/311284.html.

6. See Paul Taylor et al., *The Rising Age Gap in Economic Well-Being*, Pew Research Center, 2011.

PART IV

Way to Go, Female Entrepreneurs!

*E*ntrepreneurship is essential to U.S. economic growth. In increasing numbers, women are becoming entrepreneurs. Some women choose to become entrepreneurs in order to be their own boss or so that they will be better able to balance family and work. Others become entrepreneurs because they see a way to offer a new product or service and thus create new wealth in the U.S. economy.

The New Class of Female Entrepreneurs

The number of female entrepreneurs has been on the rise. According to the Small Business Administration (SBA), the number of women-owned nonfarm businesses rose by 11 percent between 2002 and 2008.[1] Estimates from the U.S. Census Bureau, as shown in figure 4-1, found that in 1997 there were 5.4 million firms that were majority owned (51 percent or more) by women, making up 26 percent of total privately owned firms. In 2002 there were 6.5 million firms that were majority owned by women, making up 28 percent of the total privately owned firms. By 2008, 7.2 million firms were majority owned by women and represented about 28 percent of all privately owned firms.[2, 3, 4]

In 2008, the Center for Women's Business Research (CWBR), a nonprofit that promotes female entrepreneurship, reported that the number of firms which are "jointly owned or at least 50 percent owned by women" had risen to over 10 million, accounting for about 40 percent of the total privately owned firms in the country.[5] The CWBR numbers are higher than those in the U.S. Census as the Census

FIGURE 4-1

Number of Women-Owned Businesses, 1997, 2002, and 2008

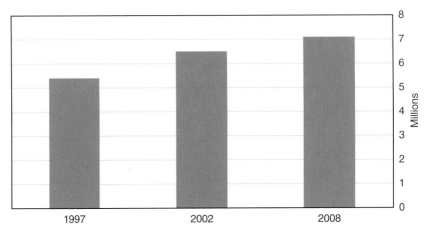

NOTE: Women-owned businesses are defined as firms in which women own at least 51 percent of interest or stocks in business.

SOURCES: Center for Women's Business Research, Biennial Update 2008: Businesses Owned by Women in the United States; U.S. Census Bureau, 1997 Survey of Women Business Enterprise; 2002 Survey of Business Owners.

defines majority owned as 51 percent or more, whereas CWBR includes firms which are only 50 percent owned by women. The CWBR also found 7.2 million firms were 51 percent or more owned by women.[6]

In 2007, the latest year for which data are available, 81 percent of all women business-owners claimed White heritage, 11 percent African American, 10 percent Hispanic American, 6 percent Asian American, 1.2 percent American Indian and Alaska Native, and 0.2 percent Native Hawaiian and Other Pacific Islander.[7] However, the CWBR reports that minority women represent 26 percent of all female business owners, while minority men represent less than 10 percent of all male business owners.[8] According to the 2005–2009 American Community Survey five-year estimates, during that period white men and women comprised 75 percent of the population; African Americans, Hispanic Americans, Asian Americans, American Indians and Alaska Natives, and Native and Other Pacific Islanders comprised 12 percent, 15 percent, 4 percent, 0.8 percent and 0.1 percent, respectively.[9, 10]

FIGURE 4-2

Industry Distribution of Women-Owned Firms, 2008

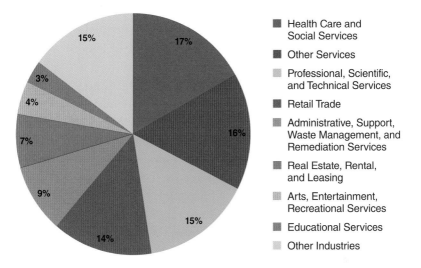

- Health Care and Social Services
- Other Services
- Professional, Scientific, and Technical Services
- Retail Trade
- Administrative, Support, Waste Management, and Remediation Services
- Real Estate, Rental, and Leasing
- Arts, Entertainment, Recreational Services
- Educational Services
- Other Industries

SOURCE: Center for Women's Business Research, Biennial Update 2008: Businesses Owned by Women in the United States.

Women entrepreneurs start businesses in a wide range of sectors. According to the CWBR, 57 percent of women-owned businesses were in the service sector in 2008.[11] As figure 4-2 shows, 17 percent of women-owned businesses offered health care and social assistance services and 15 percent offered professional, scientific, and technical services. Businesses in retail trade made up 14 percent of the total.[12]

Women-owned firms have also been receiving increasing amounts of capital in order to expand their businesses. Between the fiscal years of 2001 and 2006, the SBA increased the number of loans to women-owned businesses from 9,986 to 23,454, an increase of almost 135 percent. The total amount of dollars loaned increased by 70 percent, from $2 billion in 2001 to $3.4 billion in 2006.[13]

The growth of entrepreneurship among women has not only given women a new source of employment and a way to improve their economic standing—it has also been a boon to the U.S. economy. According to a 2006 SBA report, in 2002 the 14 percent of firms in the United States that were women-owned employer firms employed about 7.1 million workers. These firms accounted for 6.5 percent of total employment and generated about $173.7 billion in annual payroll.[14] A 2008 CWBR report estimated that majority women-owned firms employed about 7.3 million workers and generated $1.1 trillion in annual revenues in 2008. When firms that are at least 50 percent owned by women are included, these firms employed a total of 13 million workers and generated $1.9 trillion in total annual revenue.[15] A 2009 study published by the CWBR sought to demonstrate the full effect of women-owned business in America by including not only direct revenues and employment, but also the effects on the rest of the economy, such that the wages paid to employees are spent in the economy which creates jobs in other sectors. It shows that an estimated 8 million majority women-owned firms have created or maintained 23 million jobs, comprising 16 percent of all jobs, and have contributed nearly $3 trillion to the U.S. economy.[16]

Reasons for Growth

Many studies have analyzed the rise in entrepreneurship among women. While some argue that the phenomenon is a result of women's search for more challenging and rewarding endeavors, others point toward their desire for more flexible work schedules, less job stress, and a way to avoid hitting the "glass ceiling."

The latter explanation is offered by Pamela Kephart and Lillian Schumacher of the University of Saint Francis, who claim that women became entrepreneurs in order to crack through the "glass ceiling."[17] Likewise, Stephan Weiler and Alexandra Bernasek of Colorado State University write that women who have the potential, motivation, and experience to move up in the formal labor market have higher returns to their skill sets when self-employed,[18] and Mary C. Mattis of Simmons College argues that women who leave corporate careers do so because of the persistent barriers to progress in the workplace.[19]

However, there are other plausible accounts of why women become entrepreneurs that do not rely upon doubtful hypotheses of discrimination against women. The rise in the number of women entrepreneurs has occurred in part because more women aspire to be in business. The percentage of MBAs conferred on women rose considerably between 1970 and 2009, such that women now earn about 45 percent of business degrees. Many female MBA students, like male MBA students, aspire to start their own businesses, and other businesswomen, who did not have the aspiration early in their careers to start businesses, quit their jobs in mid-career to fill in profitable market opportunities that arise.[20]

Many women become entrepreneurs to engage in challenging work for self-fulfillment. The desire for a flexible work schedule is another reason for the growth in women entrepreneurs. Mattis's study found that 22 percent of the respondents who quit their jobs to start their own business did so for the independence and self-fulfillment there is in being one's own boss, while 44 percent did so for a more flexible schedule.[21]

It seems that "cracking the glass ceiling" depends more on women's skill level, qualifications, and experience than on overcoming purported discrimination. Without the necessary experience, qualifications and skills, women entrepreneurs are likely to face glass ceilings in expanding their businesses as well. There is some evidence that women fear that they suffer from such barriers. Robert D. Hisrich of Boston College and Candida Brush of H&P Associates found that women entrepreneurs typically believed that they lacked management skills in the areas of finance, marketing and planning, and most claimed that they lacked financial planning skills in their start-up phases.[22]

Moreover, many women's desire for flexibility in their work may come at a cost. Lois M. Shelton of Chapman University found that work-family management strategies are crucial determinants of business growth for women, and that women with high-growth ventures have less work-family conflict than do less-successful women.[23] Although work flexibility may be convenient and important for families, it is not conducive to business growth unless well managed. However, high growth is not necessary to all women entrepreneurs. Women who are so-called "lifestyle entrepreneurs" and who find that their business provides them with interesting work, some income, and time for their families do not need to be featured as a *Harvard Business Review* case study to feel that they are successful businesswomen.

Room for More Growth

Although 40 percent of all women-owned firms report that they want to grow as big as possible, only 3 percent of these firms generate more than $1 million in annual revenues, in contrast to 6 percent of all men-owned firms.[24]

There are a number of barriers to growth. The National Association of Women Business Owners found in a 2010 survey of its membership that education and workforce development, federal procurement, and work-life balance are among the top concerns for women entrepreneurs.[25] The federal procurement process is not simple, involving much paperwork and a detailed familiarity with individual agencies. As discussed just above, financial planning and management skills also seem to be the significant barriers to business expansion and management.

The same survey also concluded that female entrepreneurs, like their male counterparts, have concerns about barriers to entrepreneurs' plans for business expansion. These included taxes, affordable healthcare, retirement benefits, and access to capital.

Numbers of female entrepreneurs will continue to grow. The Internet is making it easier to start and operate businesses and to work from home. It is now simpler to get suppliers and find customers, both domestically and from overseas. As the economy improves, entrepreneurship, both male and female, will continue its upward path.

NOTES

1. U.S. Small Business Administration, Office of Advocacy, *Women in Business: 2009. A Demographic Review of Women's Business Ownership*, 2009.

2. U.S. Census Bureau, *1997 Economic Census: Women Owned Businesses,* 2001 http://www2.census.gov/econ/sbo/97/e97cs-2.pdf (accessed September 12, 2011): 12.

3. U.S. Census Bureau, *Survey of Business Owners—Women-Owned Firms,* 2002 http://www.census.gov/econ/sbo/02/womensof.html (accessed September 8, 2011).

4. U.S. Small Business Administration, Office of Advocacy, *Women in Business: A Demographic Review of Women's Business Ownership*, August 2006. http://archive. sba.gov/advo/research/rs280tot.pdf.

5. Center for Women's Business Research, *Biennial Update 2008: Businesses Owned by Women in the United States*, 2008, http://www.sba.gov/advo/researchrs280tot.pdf.

6. *Key Facts*. Center for Women's Business Research, 2009, http://www.womens businessresearchcenter.org/research/keyfacts/ (accessed September 26, 2011.)

7. U.S. Small Business Administration, Office of Advocacy, 2006.

8. Center for Women's Business Research, 2008.

9. U.S. Census Bureau, American Community Survey 2005–2009, http://factfinder. census.gov/servlet/DTTable?_bm=y&-geo_id=01000US&-ds_name=ACS_2009_ 5YR_G00_&-redoLog=false&-mt_name=ACS_2009_ 5YR_G2000_ B02001 (accessed September 26, 2011).

10. U.S. Census Bureau, American Community Survey 2005–2009, http://factfinder. census.gov/servlet/DTTable?_bm=y&-geo_id=01000US&-ds_name=ACS_2009_ 5YR_G00_&-redoLog=false&-mt_name=ACS_2009_ 5YR_G2000_ B03001 (accessed September 26, 2011).

11. Ibid.

12. Ibid.

13. U.S. Small Business Administration, The Facts on SBA Loans to Minorities and Women 2007, news release, May 9, 2007, http://www.sba.gov/news/pressmain/ index.html.

14. Ibid.

15. Center for Women's Business Research, 2008.

16. Center for Women's Business Research, *The Economic Impact of Women-Owned Businesses in the United States*, 2009, http://www.womensbusinessresearchcenter. org/Data/research/economicimpactstud/econimpactreport-final.pdf.

17. Pamela Kephart and Lillian Schumacher, "Has the 'Glass Ceiling' Cracked? An Exploration of Women Entrepreneurship," *Journal of Leadership & Organizational Studies* 12, no. 2 (2005): 2–16.

18. Stephan Weiler and Alexandra Bernasek, "Dodging the Glass Ceiling? Networks and the New Wave of Women Entrepreneurs," *The Social Science Journal* 38, no. 1 (2001): 85–103.

19. Mary C. Mattis, "Women Entrepreneurs: Out From Under the Glass Ceiling," *Women in Management Review* 19.3 (2004): 154.

20. Weiler and Bernasek, "Dodging the Glass Ceiling?"

21. Mattis, "Women Entrepreneurs."

22. Robert Hisrich and Candida Brush, "The Woman Entrepreneur: Management Skills and Business Problems," *Journal of Small Business Management* 22, no. 1 (1984): 30–38.

23. Lois M. Shelton, "Female Entrepreneurs, Work Family Conflict, and Venture Performance: New Insights into the Work-Family Interface," *Journal of Small Business Management* 44, no. 2 (2006): 285–98.

24. Center for Women's Business Research, "Guide for Financing Business Growth Offers Actionable Advice for Women Business Owners," news release, April 4, 2007, http://www.womensbusinessresearch.com/press/details.php?id=156.

25. National Association of Women Business Owners, "2010 Policy Priorities of Women Business Owners," *National Women's Business Council*, September 22, 2004.

PART
V

The Success of Minority Women

*A*ll groups of women have made economic progress since 1970, but the achievements of African American, Hispanic American, and Asian American women have been especially remarkable. Many of these women have overcome the obstacles in education and the labor market, and in addition have faced greater social barriers due to their race.

Minority Women in the Workforce

As this section describes, each group of minority women faces different situations vis-à-vis white women and vis-à-vis men within their same group.

African American Women. Over the last few decades, African American women have broken through gender and race barriers to build their careers. The wage gap between African American men and women has been consistently smaller than that between white men and women in the past three decades, as shown in figure 5-1. The Bureau of Labor Statistics estimates that in 2010 African American women earned fully 94 cents for every dollar earned by African American men, using median weekly earnings of full-time wage and salary workers, even without accounting for differences in education, experience, and occupation.[1]

The smaller wage gap between African American men and women partly reflects women's higher educational achievement compared to African American men. Figure 5-2 shows that African

FIGURE 5-1

Women's Median Usual Weekly Earnings as a Percentage of Men's by Race and Ethnicity, 1979–2010

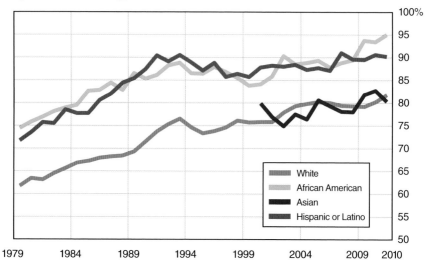

SOURCES: U.S. Department of Labor, Bureau of Labor Statistics, *Women in the Labor Force: A Databook* (2009), table 16; *Employment and Earnings* (January 2010), annual averages, table 37.

FIGURE 5-2

Women's Share of College Degrees Awarded to African Americans, 1977–2009

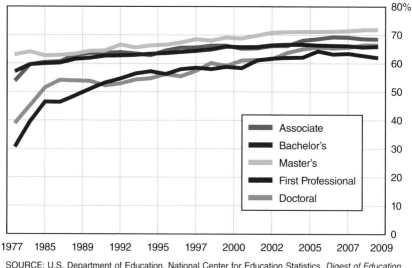

SOURCE: U.S. Department of Education, National Center for Education Statistics, *Digest of Education Statistics 2009* (2010).

FIGURE 5-3

African American Labor Force Participation Rates by Sex, 1972–2011

NOTE: Ages 16 and over.

SOURCE: U.S. Department of Labor, Bureau of Labor Statistics, Current Population Survey.

American women have earned more than half of all associate's, bachelor's and master's degrees awarded to African Americans over the past 30 years. African American women have likewise become more likely than African American men to earn advanced degrees. In 1977 just over 30 percent of professional degrees and about 40 percent of doctoral degrees among African Americans were awarded to women, but in 2009, women's share had increased to 62 percent of professional degrees and more than 66 percent of doctoral degrees.

The labor force participation rate of African American women has increased significantly over the past three decades, as shown in figure 5-3. A comparison of participation rates of African American men and women shows that the percentage of women in the labor force has been steadily increasing over the years, even while the percentage of African American men in the labor force has been declining. In 1972, the labor force participation rates of African American men and women were 74 percent and 49 percent respectively, a difference of 25 percentage points. By 2011, the difference in labor force participation rates had decreased to about 5 percentage

African American Unemployment Rates by Sex, 1972–2011

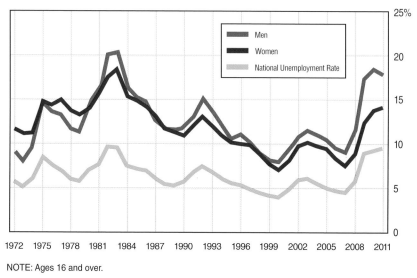

NOTE: Ages 16 and over.

SOURCE: U.S. Department of Labor, Bureau of Labor Statistics, Current Population Survey.

points, with the labor force participation rates of African American men at 64 percent and of women at 59 percent.

Figure 5-4 shows the unemployment rates for African American men and women. In the majority of the years since the 1980s, the unemployment rate of African American women has been lower than that of African American men. This trend likely exists because African American women are more highly educated than their male counterparts.

Not only have African American women been successful in closing the gender gap with African American men, but they have also narrowed historically large differences with white women. In 1953, median income for white women was more than one-and-a-half times the median income for African American women. But by 1972, the difference was only 10 percent, and by 2008, the difference was less than 4 percent. During the recent economic downturn the gap has once again widened. In 2009 the gap between white and African American women had grown to about 8 percent, with white women earning a median income of $21,118 and African American women earning a median income of $19,407, as shown in figure 5-5.

FIGURE 5-5

Women's Median Income by Race and Ethnicity (2009 dollars), 1948–2009

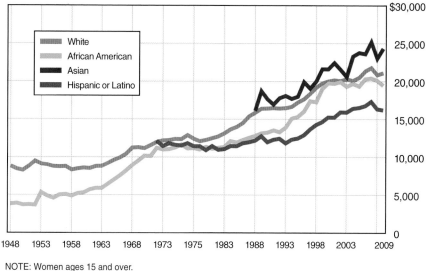

NOTE: Women ages 15 and over.

SOURCE: U.S. Census Bureau, Current Population Survey, Annual Social and Economic Supplements.

Hispanic American Women. In 1979, Hispanic American women earned 72 cents for every dollar earned by Hispanic men. Since then, Hispanic women have attained greater academic and career success and, by 2010, they earned 91 cents for every dollar that Hispanic men earned.[2] As with the African American wage ratio discussed above, this does not account for variations in education, occupation, and experience. If these factors are taken into account, the wage gap between Hispanic men and women is even smaller.

The closing of the wage gap between Hispanic American men and women resulted from a corresponding increase in Hispanic American women's educational achievement. In 2009, Hispanic women earned more than 60 percent of all associate's, bachelor's, and master's degrees awarded to Hispanics, as shown in figure 5-6. The increase in the percentage of first professional and doctoral degrees awarded to Hispanic women has been particularly noteworthy. In 1977, of all such degrees awarded to Hispanics, only 17 percent of first professional degrees and 27 percent of doctoral

FIGURE 5-6

Women's Share of College Degrees Awarded to Hispanic Americans, 1977–2009

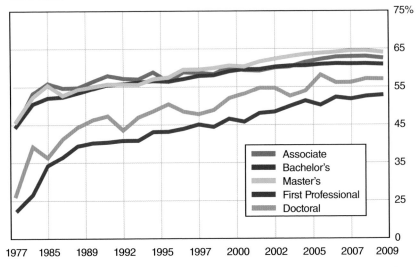

SOURCE: U.S. Department of Education, National Center for Education Statistics, *Digest of Education Statistics 2009* (2010).

FIGURE 5-7

Hispanic American Labor Force Participation by Sex, 1973–2011

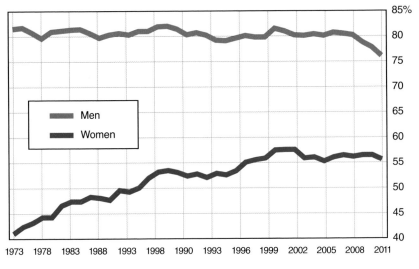

NOTE: Ages 16 and over.

SOURCE: U.S. Department of Labor, Bureau of Labor Statistics, Current Population Survey.

degrees were conferred on Hispanic women. By 2009, Hispanic women received more than 50 percent of first professional and doctoral degrees awarded to Hispanics.

Historically, labor force participation rates for Hispanic women have lagged far behind those for Hispanic men. For cultural reasons, many Hispanic women have stayed home with their children and hence invested less in education. However, this has been changing in recent years, as shown in figure 5-7. In 1973, the labor force participation rate of Hispanic men was double that of Hispanic women: 81 percent of Hispanic men verses only 41 percent of Hispanic women. Yet by the beginning of 2011, the difference was almost halved. Hispanic men's labor participation rate had declined to 76 percent, whereas the rate for women had jumped to 55 percent. Many Hispanic men are employed in construction, which continues to decline even though the recession ended in June 2009. On the other hand, many Hispanic women are employed in the service sector, particularly health care and hospitality, which continues to generate jobs.

FIGURE 5-8

Hispanic American Unemployment Rates by Sex, 1973–2011

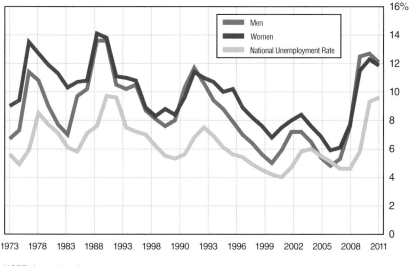

NOTE: Ages 16 and over.

SOURCE: U.S. Department of Labor, Bureau of Labor Statistics, Current Population Survey.

Unemployment rates for Hispanic women in the United States have been consistently higher than those for Hispanic men in the period 1973–2011, as shown in figure 5-8. The largest difference occurred in 1978 and 1979, when the rates for women were 3.6 and 3.3 percentage points respectively higher than the rate for men. In every other year the difference was less than 3 percentage points, and in 15 of the 37 years the difference was less than 1 percentage point. This changed in 2009, as Hispanic men were disproportionately affected by declines in construction and blue collar employment and Hispanic women employed in services fared better. In 2009, the unemployment rate for Hispanic women was 11 percent, a whole percentage point lower than men's unemployment rate of 12 percent. In 2011 the gap between unemployment rates for Hispanic women and men remained about a percentage point.

Although Hispanic women started out with earnings on par with white women, about $12,000 annually in 1972, as seen in figure 5-5, Hispanic women's earnings declined and stagnated at around

FIGURE 5-9

Women's Share of College Degrees Awarded to Asian Americans, 1977–2009

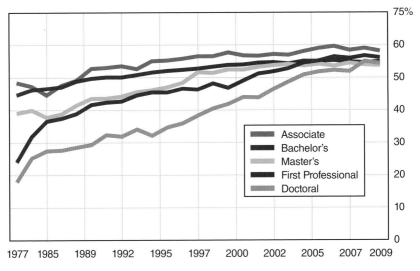

SOURCE: U.S. Department of Education, National Center for Education Statistics, *Digest of Education Statistics 2009* (2010).

FIGURE 5-10

Asian American Labor Force Participation Rates by Sex, 2000–2011

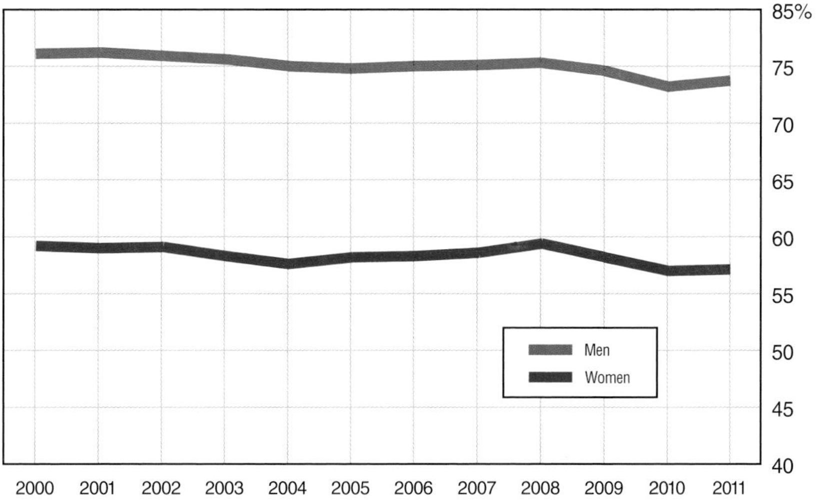

NOTE: Ages 16 and over.

SOURCE: U.S. Department of Labor, Bureau of Labor Statistics, Current Population Survey.

$11,000 from the early 1970s to the mid-1980s. In 1993 Hispanic women's earnings were still $12,000 annually, but then they started increasing at the same rate as white women's. Ten years later in 2003, Hispanic women were making $16,000 while white women were making $20,000, making the gap 20 percent. After women's wages across ethnicities peaked in 2007, the gap between Hispanic women and white women is currently just under 25 percent.

Asian American Women. For every dollar earned by Asian American men, Asian American women earned 83 cents in 2010, without accounting for differences in education, experience, and time in the workforce.[3] Asian American women's earning have fluctuated between 75 and 82 percent of Asian American men's earnings since 2000. Although Asian American women earned much less than their male counterparts, the median incomes of Asian American women have been consistently higher than women in any other racial or ethnic group since 2002, according to estimates provided by the U.S. Census Bureau.

FIGURE 5-11

Asian American Unemployment Rates by Sex, 2000–2011

NOTE: Ages 16 and over.

SOURCE: U.S. Department of Labor, Bureau of Labor Statistics, Current Population Survey.

As with women of other backgrounds, Asian American women have been earning academic degrees at rates that exceed those of men. This is most apparent in the number of doctoral degrees conferred to Asian women. In 1977 only 18 percent of doctoral degrees earned by Asian Americans were conferred on women, but by 2009 this number increased to 54 percent, as seen in figure 5-9.

Over the last decade, Asian American women had a labor force participation rate about 17 percentage points lower than Asian American men, as shown in figure 5-10. The male-female gap in labor force participation is significantly higher for Asian Americans than it is for African Americans, but lower than it is for Hispanics.

In the period 2000–2011, unemployment rates for Asian American men and women have been very close, as seen in figure 5-11. The rates differed by more than one percentage point only in 2009, when women's unemployment was 1.3 percentage points lower than men's. As with other groups, Asian American women had a lower unemployment rate than Asian American men for most of the last decade, reflecting the higher employment of women in the service sector.

In 1987 Asian American women were earning the same amount as white women, $16,000 annually as seen in Figure 5-5. Asian American women quickly overtook white women in earnings, with the gap between the two hitting its maximum in 2004 when Asian American women made $24,000 in comparison with white women's $20,000, a gap of 20 percent. Asian American women's earnings peaked in 2007 at $25,000. As of 2009, Asian American women made $24,000 while white women made $21,000, bringing the gap to approximately 12 percent.

Minority Women as Working Mothers and Business Leaders

Minority women are increasingly likely to work while they have young children and to be entrepreneurs and business leaders.

FIGURE 5-12

Mothers' Labor Force Participation Rates, 1996–2010

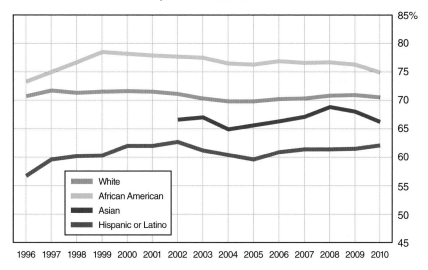

SOURCE: U.S. Department of Labor, Bureau of Labor Statistics, *Labor Force Characteristics by Race and Ethnicity 2009* (2010), table 2, table 9.

Minority Women as Working Mothers. Changes in cultural attitudes and improvements in technology have contributed to mothers' ability to work. In the period 1996–2010, as shown in figure 5-12, labor force participation rates by white mothers remained fairly constant at 71 percent. Those of minority mothers increased from 73 percent to 75 percent for African American women and from 57 percent to 62 percent for Hispanic women. In 2010, labor force participation rates for Asian American mothers were 67 percent. They were 62 percent for Hispanic mothers, and 75 percent for African American mothers.

These differing labor force participation rates are influenced by family demographics. African American mothers are the most likely to participate in the labor force, and are also the most likely to lead their families without a husband. Almost half of African American families are headed by single mothers. The Bureau of Labor Statistics reported that in 2009, 44 percent of African American families, compared to 25 percent of Hispanic families, 15 percent of white families, and 13 percent of Asian American families, were headed by

FIGURE 5-13

Ratio of Women to Men in Management, Professional, and Related Occupations by Race, 1994–2010

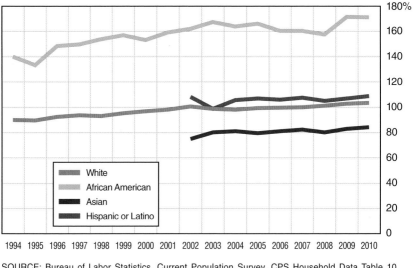

SOURCE: Bureau of Labor Statistics, Current Population Survey, CPS Household Data Table 10 (1994–2010).

women without a spouse.[4] However, the presence of a spouse is not necessarily the main factor contributing to a mother's decision to participate in the labor force. Hispanic mothers as a group are the second most likely to lead their families without a husband but are the least likely to remain in the workforce.

Minority Women in Management and Business. Another way of gauging minority women's progress in the workforce is to look at data on their employment in traditionally higher-paid and more prestigious occupations, such as the management, business, and financial operations sector. Minority women are breaking down barriers in the workforce. Not only are they moving ahead in terms of employment and labor participation rates, but they are also increasingly moving into management, business, and financial operations.

FIGURE 5-14

Women Employed in Management, Business, and Financial Operations Occupations as a Percentage of the Total Number of Employed Women by Race, 1994–2010

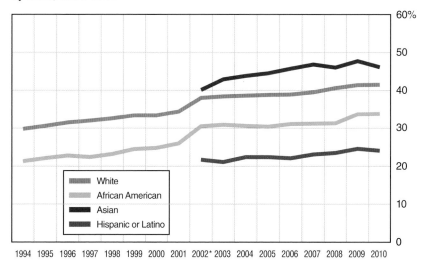

*The sharp rise in 2002 can be explained by the introduction of changes in reporting race groups beginning 2003.

SOURCE: Bureau of Labor Statistics, Current Population Survey, CPS Household Data Table 10 (1995–2010).

Data for the period 1994–2010 show that the number of female African American employees has exceeded the number of African American male employees in this sector every year over the last sixteen years. For the 2002–2010 period, increasing proportions of white, Hispanic, and Asian American women were employed in management and professional occupations. Eight percent more Hispanic women are employed in these high-paying occupations than Hispanic men. White women are shown to have reversed the gap by 2009, at which point they represented just over half of whites in this sector. The gap is currently largest for Asian American women, though they too are showing increases as shown in figure 5-13.

The proportion of employed women in management, business, and financial operations increased slightly in the first decade of the twenty-first century despite the recession, as illustrated in figure 5-14. Asian American women have been working in this sector in the highest proportion, followed by white, African American, and Hispanic women. In 2002, 40 percent of all employed Asian American women worked in management, business, and financial operations occupations. By 2010, this number stood at 46 percent, although it peaked in 2009 at 48 percent. In the same time period, the proportion of all employed white women working in this sector grew from 38 percent to 41.5 percent. For African American women it rose from 30 to 34 percent, and from 21 percent to 24 percent for Hispanic women.[5]

NOTES

1. U.S. Department of Labor, Bureau of Labor Statistics, *Women in the Labor Force: A Databook,* Report 1034, (2010), 51.

2. U.S. Department of Labor, Bureau of Labor Statistics, *Highlights of Women's Earnings in 2010.* 2011. http://www.bls.gov/cps/cpswom2010.pdf (accessed September 14, 2011).

3. Ibid.

4. U.S. Department of Labor, Bureau of Labor Statistics, *Labor Force Characteristics by Race and Ethnicity,* 2008, http://www.bls.gov/cps/cpsrace2009.pdf.

5. U.S. Department of Labor, Bureau of Labor Statistics, *Employed Persons by Occupation, Race and Hispanic or Latino Ethnicity, and Sex, 2010.* http://www.bls.gov/cps/cpsaat10.pdf.

PART
VI

Mirror, Mirror, on the Wall, Which Country Is the Fairest of Them All?

*A*t the same time as American women have made great strides in higher education, the workforce, and business, women in other developed economies, as well as in developing economies like Mexico, have made progress that parallels that of American women. This chapter analyzes the changes in labor force participation, unemployment, and higher education of American women in a comparative context.

It is clear that the changes that have affected American women are part of global changes in women's roles. Women's labor force participation rates have shown remarkable increases. Women's unemployment rates tend to be comparable to or lower than men's. Women are a majority of students receiving degrees, and women are waiting longer to have their first child and having fewer children in total, allowing them to take fewer career breaks and spend more time on work outside the home. These remarkable changes have led to great improvements in women's opportunities over the last half-century.

Labor Force Participation and Unemployment

The labor force participation rates of women around the world have increased substantially over the past decades, in large part because cultural and technological changes have enabled women to combine work and family more easily. Figure 6-1 presents labor force participation rates between 1970 and 2010 for a select group of ten Organisation for Economic Co-operation and Development (OECD) countries: the United States, the United Kingdom, Sweden, the Netherlands, Italy, Germany, France, Japan, Australia, and Canada.

Women's labor force participation has increased in all these countries except Japan. In 1970, as shown in table 6-1, the highest rate recorded was in Sweden, with a labor force participation rate of 50 percent. In that same year, Italy roughly had only a quarter of women participate in their labor force. By 2010, these rates had increased substantially. In Canada, the labor force participation rate for women was the highest at 62 percent. Sweden, at 60 percent, and the Netherlands and the United States, both at 58 percent, were not far behind. Italy still had the lowest percentage of the ten countries analyzed, with a rate of 38 percent.

In the first two decades of the 1970–2010 period, from 1970 to 1990, women's labor force participation rates increased dramatically, by 20 percentage points in Canada and 14 percentage points in the United States. In the second two decades of this period, from 1990 to 2010, every country except for Japan and Sweden recorded increasing participation rates of women in the labor force, although in countries such as Canada, the United States, and the United Kingdom the growth was more modest than in the 1970–1990 period. The Netherlands experienced dramatic growth in women's labor force participation throughout the 1970–2010 period. In 1973 it had one of the lowest women's participation rates at 28 percent, but this rose to 44 percent in 1990 and then to 58 percent in 2010.

In contrast to women's increased participation in the labor force, men's labor force participation rates declined between 1970 and 2010. This can be seen in table 6-1. In 1970, men's labor force participation rates in the United States, Japan, the United Kingdom, and Australia were around 80 percent. Australia had the highest labor force participation rate for men at 84 percent. By the year 2010, men's labor force participation rates had declined in each country by an average of 10 percentage points. Australia continued to enjoy the highest labor force participation rate at 73 percent, a decline of 11 percentage points since 1970. The most dramatic decrease occurred in France, with a drop of 16 percentage points. The United States had a smaller decline of 8.5 percentage points.

As countries became wealthier, more young men went to college and graduate school, and retirement ages declined. In contrast, women's labor force participation has been rising. Not only did more women enter the labor force in the 1980s, but these

FIGURE 6-1

Labor Force Participation Rates of Women

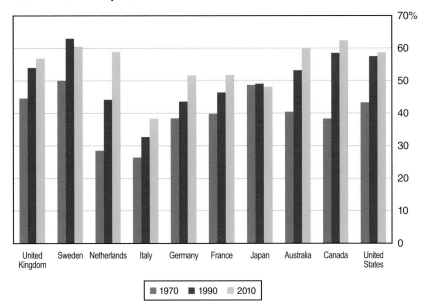

*1973 Rate for Netherlands

**1971 Rate for United Kingdom

SOURCE: U.S. Department of Labor, Bureau of Labor Statistics, Division of International Labor Comparisons, *International Comparisons of Annual Labor Force Statistics, Adjusted to U.S. Concepts, 10 Countries, 1970-2010*, Table 3-5, http://www.bls.gov/fls/flscomparelf/labor_force.htm#table3_5.

TABLE 6-1

Labor Force Participation Rates by Sex, 1970 and 2010

Country and Sex	Labor Force Participation Rates		Percentage Point Difference	Percentage Change
	1970	2010	1970–2010	1970–2010
Men				
United States	79.7	71.2	−8.5	−10.66%
Canada	77.8	71.8	−6.0	−7.71%
Australia	84.1	73.2	−10.9	−12.96%
Japan	81.5	70.8	−10.7	−13.13%
France	77.5	61.9	−15.6	−20.13%
Germany	78.7	65.1	−13.6	−17.28%
Italy	73.7	59.1	−14.6	−19.81%
Netherlands	79.4	69.9	−9.5	−11.96%
Sweden	78.5	69.1	−9.4	−11.97%
United Kingdom	83.1	69.9	−13.2	−15.88%
Women				
United States	43.3	58.6	15.3	35.33%
Canada	38.3	62.4	24.1	62.92%
Australia	40.4	59.8	19.4	48.02%
Japan	48.7	48.1	−0.6	−1.23%
France	39.8	51.7	11.9	29.90%
Germany	38.4	51.6	13.2	34.38%
Italy	26.4	38.3	11.9	45.08%
Netherlands	28.5	58.8	30.3	106.32%
Sweden	50.0	60.4	10.4	20.80%
United Kingdom	44.6	56.8	12.2	27.35%

SOURCE: U.S. Department of Labor, Bureau of Labor Statistics, Division of International Labor Comparisons, *International Comparisons of Annual Labor Force Statistics, Adjusted to U.S. Concepts, 10 Countries, 1970–2010,* Tables 3–4 and 3–5.

women are staying in the workforce through retirement. Women are investing in education with the goal of a lifetime career, rather than just a few years in the workforce.

The unemployment trends for women in this group of ten OECD countries have varied widely over the past 30 years, reflecting

FIGURE 6-2

Unemployment Rates for Women, 2010

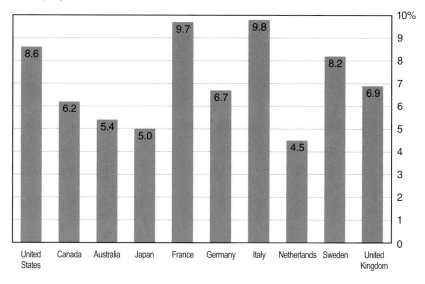

SOURCE: U.S. Department of Labor, Bureau of Labor Statistics, Division of International Labor Comparisons, *International Comparisons of Annual Labor Force Statistics, Adjusted to U.S. Concepts, 10 Countries, 1970-2010,* Table 1-4.

economic conditions in individual countries. In 1970, the United States had a relatively higher unemployment rate for women. By 2008, the female unemployment rate in the United States was lower than in most European countries in this group but higher than in Australia, Canada, and Japan.[1] But by the end of 2010, the unemployment rate for U.S. women has exceeded the rates for women in the European countries except for France and Italy. At the end of 2010, as shown in figure 6-2, unemployment rates for women were highest in Italy, France, and United States with percentages of 9.8, 9.7, and 8.6 respectively. The Netherlands, Japan, and Australia had the lowest unemployment rates with percentages of 4.5, 5.0, and 5.4 for women.

As shown in table 6-2, women had lower unemployment rates than men in the United States, Canada, Germany, the United Kingdom, and Sweden. In the United States the women's unemployment rates were 1.9 percentage points below men's rates. Women are doing better than men in the latest recession, because they are benefiting from service sector jobs. In contrast, men have been

TABLE 6-2

Unemployment Rates by Sex, 2010

Country	Unemployment Rates		Percentage Point Difference
	Men	Women	
United States	10.5%	8.6%	1.9
Canada	7.8%	6.2%	1.6
Australia	5.1%	5.4%	−0.3
Japan	4.6%	5.0%	−0.4
France	9.2%	9.7%	−0.5
Germany	7.7%	6.7%	1.0
Italy	7.7%	9.8%	−2.1
Netherlands	4.5%	4.5%	0.0
Sweden	8.4%	8.2%	0.2
United Kingdom	8.7%	6.9%	1.8

SOURCE: U.S. Department of Labor, Bureau of Labor Statistics, Division of International Labor Comparisons, 2011.

affected by the decline in the construction and manufacturing sectors. Equal unemployment rates of 4.5 percent for men and women were observed in the Netherlands. In the other four countries analyzed, men had lower unemployment rates than women. The largest gap in unemployment rates between men and women in 2010 occurred in Italy with a difference of 2.1 percentage points.

International Fertility Rates

Fertility rates internationally have been decreasing at a substantial rate since the 1960s. The OECD determines a country's fertility rate in a specific year by calculating the number of children that would be born to each woman if she were to live to the end of her childbearing years and if she gave birth to children at each age at the currently prevailing age-specific fertility rate.[2] Figure 6-3 shows how fertility rates have declined in a group of OECD countries that includes Australia, Canada, France, Germany, Italy, Japan, Korea,

FIGURE 6-3

Total Fertility Rates, 1960, 1980, 2009

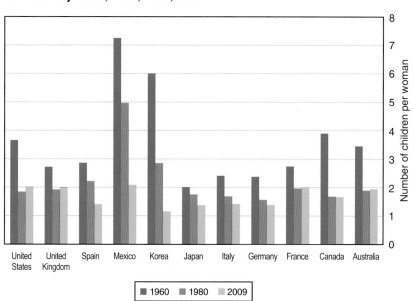

SOURCE: OECD Family Database, 2011.

Mexico, Spain, the United Kingdom, and the United States. As seen in the graph, fertility rates in the 1960s were much higher than those in 1980 and 2009. In the United States, for example, the fertility rate in 1960 was 3.65, in 1980 it was 1.84, and in 2009 it was at 2.01

As table 6-3 shows, in most countries the decline in fertility rates was much greater in the two decades from 1960 to 1980 than in the following three decades from 1980 to 2009. Between 1960 and 1980 Canada had the largest decrease in its fertility rate, with a decline of 2.22 births per woman, or a percentage decrease of 57 percent. Korea and the United States also had large declines, with fertility rate declines of 3.18 (a decrease of 53 percent) and 1.81 (a decrease of 50 percent) respectively. Countries experiencing the smallest decreases in fertility rates between 1960 and 1980 were Japan with a decrease of 0.25, or 13 percent; Spain with a decrease of 0.65, or 23 percent; and France with a decrease of 0.79, or 29 percent.

TABLE 6-3

Percentage Change in Fertility Rates

Country	Percentage Change in Fertility		
	1960–1980	1980–2009	1960–2009
Australia	−45.2%	0.5%	−44.9%
Canada	−56.9%	−1.2%	−57.4%
France	−29.0%	2.3%	−27.4%
Germany	−34.0%	−11.8%	−42.6%
Italy	−30.1%	−16.3%	−41.4%
Japan	−12.5%	−21.7%	−31.5%
Korea	−53.0%	−59.2%	−80.8%
Mexico	−31.4%	−58.1%	−71.3%
Spain	−22.6%	−36.8%	−51.0%
United Kingdom	−30.1%	2.1%	−28.7%
United States	−49.7%	9.3%	−45.0%

SOURCE: Organisation for Economic Co–operation and Development, *OECD Family Database* (2011).

From 1980 to 2009, only Australia, France, the United Kingdom, and the United States experienced increasing fertility rates. In this subset of countries, all except for the United States had relatively small increases in their fertility rates, with an average increase of 3.5 percent. The United States, however, had an increase of 9 percent, or 0.17 births per woman. Canada, Germany, Italy, Japan, Korea, Mexico, and Spain again experienced falling fertility rates. Korea and Mexico had the largest decline in fertility rates, with a decrease of 58 percent in Mexico and 59 percent in Korea. Spain also experienced a significant decrease of 37 percent.

Global fertility has declined over the last half-century. This is especially true in countries that have experienced rapid economic development. For example, since 1960 Korea has experienced an 80 percent decrease in fertility, as women went from having an average of six children to just one child. Over the same period, Mexico experienced a 71 percent decline in fertility as women went from having an average of seven children to only two. In comparison, the United States fertility rate has not fallen as drastically, but has still seen a large decrease of 44.2 percent since 1960. American women on average had one fewer child in 2009 than they did in 1960 (which partly explains why our Social Security and Medicare programs are out of balance). The picture is similar to that of Canada, Australia, the United Kingdom, Spain, Italy, and Germany. French women, on the other hand, had a relatively low fertility rate in 1960 of 2.74, and have only seen a decline in fertility of 28 percent. Japan, likewise, has seen a decline of only 31.5 percent, though it started out with a fertility rate of only 2.0 in 1960, at a time when the United States had a fertility rate of over 3.5.

By 2009 most of these countries described above had a fertility rate of equal to or less than 2 births per woman. The only exceptions were the United States and Mexico with rates of 2.08 and 2.04 births per woman respectively. Each country has fallen or is close to falling below the "replacement level of fertility" of 2.1 children per woman, which the OECD considers to be the replacement level of fertility as it generates broad stability of the population.[3]

In tandem with declining fertility, the average age of mothers at the birth of their first child has been rising, as seen in figures 6-4 and 6-5. In Japan, Korea, Spain, Italy, Germany, and the United Kingdom, a woman became a mother on average at the age of 29 or 30 in 2008. Women in Canada, Australia, and France tended to have their first child at the ages of 27 or 28. The United States and Mexico reported lower average ages of mothers, with women becoming mothers at ages 25 and 21 respectively.

With fewer children and a longer period to complete their studies and establish themselves in careers before they become mothers, women are spending more time on paid work outside the home. Women are more able to move up the corporate ladder and to choose careers in innovative and lucrative fields. Nevertheless, motherhood does slow career advancement and limit employment. The OECD reports that there is a negative relationship between female employment and fertility rates but also that the correlation differs across OECD countries.

To judge from data presented in figure 6-6, combining work and children is most difficult in Japan and Italy, as can be seen from the lower labor force participation rates of 48.1 and 38.3, respectively.

FIGURE 6-4

Mean Age of Women at the Birth of First Child, 1995

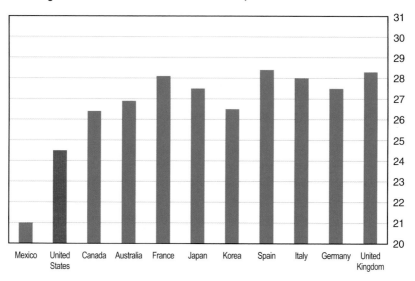

SOURCE: Organisation for Economic Co-operation and Development, *OECD Family Database* (2011).

FIGURE 6-5

Mean Age of Women at the Birth of First Child, 2008

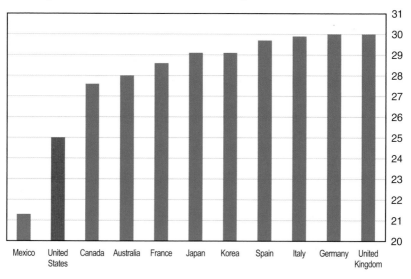

SOURCE: Organisation for Economic Co-operation and Development, *OECD Family Database* (2011).

FIGURE 6-6

Women's Labor Force Participation Rates, 2010

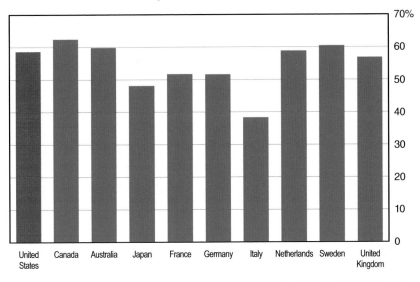

SOURCE: Bureau of Labor Statistics: International Comparisons of Annual Labor Force Statistics, Adjusted to U.S. Concepts, 10 Countries, 1970-2010.

But it has been less difficult in countries like the United States, Canada, Australia, the Netherlands, and Sweden, where labor force participation rates for women are higher.[4]

Higher Education

Education is crowding out children. The best form of birth control is a college degree, not just because of the time it takes, but also because of the work opportunities it provides afterward. As women are now the majority of higher education students in the United States, so are women the majority of higher education students in other OECD countries.

Figure 6-7 shows the women's share of students enrolled in higher education for the years 2000 and 2005 as well as projections for the year 2015. In 2000, women made up the majority of students in higher education in Australia, Canada, France, Italy, Sweden, Spain, the United Kingdom, and the United States. Women were enrolled

FIGURE 6-7

Women's Share of Students in Higher Education, 2000, 2005, and 2015

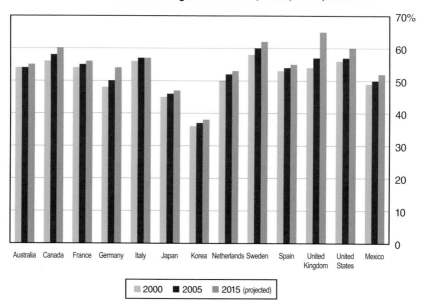

SOURCE: Organisation for Economic Co-operation and Development, *Higher Education to 2030, vol. 1, Demography* (2008).

in equal numbers to men in the Netherlands, and they remained a minority of students in Germany, Mexico, Japan, and Korea. By the year 2005, numbers of women and men enrolled at the university and college level were equal in Mexico and Germany, but women still lagged behind men in Japan and Korea. From 2000 to 2005, each country showed increases in the percentages of women students enrolled in colleges and universities. Projections for the year 2015 show this trend.

With women the majority of students in post-secondary education, they are becoming the majority of higher education graduates. Figure 6-8 shows that, with the exception of Japan and Korea, women graduated at higher percentages than men in these selected OECD countries. It is interesting to note, however, that in 2005 women in Korea and Japan were respectively 37 and 46 percent of college students but women were fully 49 percent of college graduates in both

FIGURE 6-8

Women's Share of College Degrees, 2005 and 2015

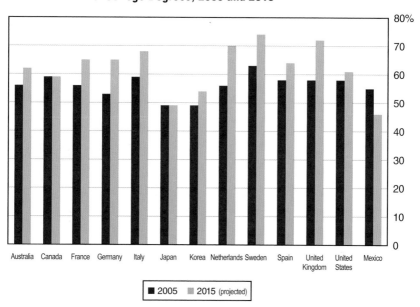

SOURCE: Organisation for Economic Co-operation and Development, *Higher Education to 2030, vol. 1, Demography* (2008).

countries. Projections for 2015 show that in the Netherlands, Sweden, and the United Kingdom, women graduates are estimated to comprise at least 70 percent of students earning degrees.

Male and female students are concentrated in different fields of study, as may be seen in table 6-4. Men and women enroll in similar numbers in the social sciences, business, and law. Women were the majority of students in the education, arts and humanities, and health and social sector fields; and men were a majority in science and engineering.

TABLE 6-4

Percentage Distribution of College Degrees by Sex and Subject, 2008

	Education	Arts and Humanities	Social Sciences, Business and Law	Sciences	Engineering	Agronomy	Health and Social Sector	Services
Female								
Australia	14.7	12.3	39.5	7.6	3.0	0.7	19.4	2.6
Canada	14.5	14.2	37.2	11.5	3.5	0.8	14.5	3.7
France	3.2	19.1	46.8	9.8	6.9	0.9	10.5	2.8
Germany	12.3	28.7	25.7	13.2	5.0	1.4	11.4	2.3
Italy	8.9	20.5	34.0	6.3	8.4	1.4	17.9	2.6
Japan	9.3	31.0	30.7	3.1	5.6	3.3	11.4	5.6
Korea	16.0	27.3	21.3	7.9	11.0	1.3	12.5	2.8
Mexico	18.7	4.3	45.7	8.1	7.5	1.2	11.4	3.0
Netherlands	21.6	8.7	34.4	2.2	2.4	1.3	24.2	5.1
Spain	20.1	9.4	29.0	6.9	7.9	1.8	20.3	4.4
Sweden	24.4	5.3	22.8	4.9	7.6	0.6	33.5	0.9
United Kingdom	13.3	19.7	33.4	9.3	3.7	0.9	18.4	1.4
United States	16.4	16.0	37.6	6.6	2.3	0.9	14.8	5.4
Male								
Australia	6.7	8.7	44.6	16.7	12.0	0.8	7.8	2.7
Canada	6.5	11.6	39.9	17.0	16.6	0.8	4.3	3.3
France	1.5	8.9	35.5	18.8	21.0	0.9	9.0	4.4
Germany	5.5	12.7	29.0	20.7	21.7	1.6	6.8	2.1
Italy	1.1	9.2	38.9	8.0	25.0	2.6	11.6	3.6
Japan	4.1	9.6	40.3	6.2	30.4	3.4	5.7	0.3
Korea	5.5	11.8	24.5	11.1	33.9	1.7	6.4	5.1
Mexico	8.7	3.7	39.3	13.2	22.7	2.8	7.3	2.2
Netherlands	6.5	8.7	41.2	11.7	14.6	1.5	10.3	5.4
Spain	7.9	8.1	28.4	14.7	24.1	2.7	9.2	4.9
Sweden	12.4	5.5	25.1	10.5	31.6	0.8	12.8	1.3
United Kingdom	5.3	15.2	34.5	19.4	15.9	0.7	7.9	1.2
United States	6.5	14.9	43.2	11.8	11.3	1.2	5.3	5.8

SOURCE: Organisation for Economic Co-operation and Development, OECD Database 2011, Education at a Glance, 2011 OECD Indicators, http://www.oecd.org/dataoecd/61/2/48631582.pdf.

NOTES

1. U.S. Department of Labor, Bureau of Labor Statistics, Division of International Labor Comparisons, *International Comparisons of Annual Labor Force Statistics, Adjusted to U.S. Concepts, 10 Countries, 1970-2010*, Table 1-4.

2. Organisation for Economic Co-operation and Development, SF2.1: Fertility Rates, *OECD Family Database* (Paris, France: Organisation for Economic Co-operation and Development, 2009), http://www.oecd.org/dataoecd/37/59/40192107.pdf.

3. Ibid. The "replacement level of fertility" ensures replacement of the couple. It is greater than 2 due to infant mortality.

3. Organisation for Economic Co-operation and Development, *Doing Better for Families, OECD Family Database* (Paris, France: Organisation for Economic Co-operation and Development, 2011), http://dx.doi.org/10.1787/9789264098732-en.

4. U.S. Department of Labor, Bureau of Labor Statistics, Division of International Labor Comparisons, *International Comparisons of Annual Labor Force Statistics, Adjusted to U.S. Concepts, 10 Countries, 1970-2010*.

PART VII

Do Feminist Organizations Serve Women Today?

*A*s we have seen in prior chapters, women currently receive around 60 percent of all associate's, bachelor's and master's degrees, and around 50 percent of first professional law, medical, dentistry, and doctoral degrees. Furthermore, although there is still an average gender wage gap of around 20 percent, according to the Bureau of Labor Statistics, this gap narrows and almost disappears once worker characteristics such as experience, time spent in the labor force, family, and career choices are taken into consideration, as discussed previously.

Despite the significant progress women have made in education and in the workplace, there is currently in America a strong advocacy movement promoting policies such as affirmative action and quotas in college admission, hiring, and federal contracting. Organizations such the National Organization for Women (NOW) and the NOW Foundation, the American Association of University Women (AAUW) Action Fund and the AAUW Educational Foundation, the National Women's Law Center (NWLC), and Catalyst promote these policies in a purported defense of women's rights.

Some of these organizations were founded early in the women's rights movement in the United States, when women truly did lag far behind men in educational and employment opportunities. Indeed, the AAUW was founded over 130 years ago, when women's economic position was far inferior to men's. Today, however, women have mostly attained equal opportunities, in some cases even surpassing men in educational and economic achievement. Not content to disband when their efforts were no longer necessary to achieve equality, these organizations continue to push for policies favoring women. By so doing, these organizations are insulting American women's efforts, accomplishments, and independence. To get a better sense of these organizations, this chapter takes a closer look at their structures, finances, and activities.

Agendas and Assets

These feminist organizations decry the gender imbalances in certain fields of study and careers. Failing to look any further than discrimination for explanations of gender disparity in the United States, they claim that gender discrimination remains a barrier to women's success in the twenty-first century. To remedy this discrimination, they conduct research, and fund women's programs. They lobby Congress, the administration, and government leaders to establish preferential programs for women in federal contracting and grant-making, to support affirmative action, to extend Title IX legislation to math and science courses, and to pass the 2011 Paycheck Fairness Act. To carry out this ambitious agenda, they have substantial assets and large operating budgets, shown in figure 7-1 and table 7-1.

These tables reveal the riches used to influence Congress's actions about legislation and programs that would supposedly benefit women. However, it is both unnecessary and unwise for lawmakers to consider legislation mandating further affirmative action and gender quotas in education, the workplace, federal contracting, grant-making, and other areas of economic life. Such legislation would risk subjecting educational institutions, private sector firms, and government agencies to additional lawsuits or decreased federal funding unless they adopt the quotas. Quotas distort these institutions' admissions, hiring, and contracting practices, thus increasing costs and lowering productivity. Quotas are unfair to men, who may be passed over for a position in favor of a less-qualified woman. They are also unfair to women because they undermine women's achievements by enforcing the belief that successful women in high positions got there through affirmative action rather than through their merit and accomplishments.

FIGURE 7-1

Revenue and Expenses of Selected Women's Organizations, 2008/2009

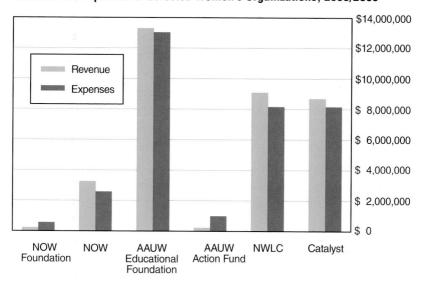

SOURCES: National Organization for Women, Inc., *U.S. Internal Revenue Service 2009 Form 990* (2010); California National Organization for Women, Inc., *U.S. Internal Revenue Service 2009 Form 990* (2010); American Association of University Women, *U.S. Internal Revenue Service 2009 Form 990* (2010); American Association of University Women, Educational Foundation, *U.S. Internal Revenue Service 2009 Form 990* (2010); National Women's Law Center, *U.S. Internal Revenue Service 2009 Form 990* (2010); and Catalyst, Inc., *U.S. Internal Revenue Service 2009 Form 990* (2010).

TABLE 7-1

Net Assets of Selected Women's Organizations, 2009

Organization	Year Founded	Net Assets (End of Year)
NOW Foundation	1986	$840,035
NOW	1966	–$661,230
AAUW Educational Foundation	1881	$111,911,193
AAUW Action Fund	1881	$2,117,382
NWLC	1972	$25,759,265
Catalyst	1962	$14,198,010
		Total = $154,164,655

SOURCES: National Organization for Women, Inc., *U.S. Internal Revenue Service 2009 Form 990* (2010); American Association of University Women, *U.S. Internal Revenue Service 2008 Form 990* (2010); National Women's Law Center, *U.S. Internal Revenue Service 2008 Form 990* (2010); and Catalyst, Inc., *U.S. Internal Revenue Service 2008 Form 990* (2010).

The National Organization for Women

The National Organization for Women is the largest feminist organization in America, bringing together over 500,000 contributing members and 500 local chapters and campus affiliates.[1] The organization was founded on June 30, 1966, and its original statement of purpose read, "The purpose of NOW is to take action to bring women into full participation in the mainstream of American society now, exercising all privileges and responsibilities thereof in truly equal partnership with men."[2] A fair assessment would conclude that this purpose has been accomplished.

Not content to rest with success, NOW has adopted new missions very different from its original one. The organization's present priorities are "pressing for an amendment to the U.S. Constitution that will guarantee equal rights for women; achieving economic equality for women; championing abortion rights, reproductive freedom, and other women's health issues; supporting civil rights for all and opposing racism; opposing bigotry against lesbians and gays; and ending violence against women."[3]

With a large budget and multiple affiliates, NOW is able to campaign for feminist activities on a number of fronts. For example, NOW is an ardent supporter of policies such as affirmative action and extending Title IX to education. These policies supposedly create equal opportunities, but in reality establish quotas and thus promote discrimination based on gender, the very kind of discrimination organizations such as NOW were founded to fight. NOW is also an ardent advocate of pay equity for women and a staunch believer that a glass ceiling prevents women from attaining top jobs.[4] As a result, NOW is a strong supporter of legislation such as the Lilly Ledbetter Fair Pay Act of 2009, which extended the period women have to sue over discrimination in pay, and the proposed Paycheck Fairness Act, which would require employers to demonstrate that differences in pay were not based on gender discrimination.[5]

Congress did not pass the Paycheck Fairness Act. Instead, the Obama administration is embarking on regulatory action to mandate equal participation in specific academic fields and career areas, and it has incorporated provisions establishing preferential treatment for women into financial and healthcare regulation.

NOW also believes that women lack adequate protection under the U.S. Constitution, and has thus been advocating for the adoption of the Equal Rights Amendment (ERA).[6] It argues that adopting the ERA is necessary because the Constitution has only explicitly guaranteed women the right to vote but other "rights not supported by the Constitution can be undermined in legislatures and courts, where women are underrepresented."[7] The ERA was originally introduced in Congress in 1923. It was passed by the House of Representatives in 1971 and then by the Senate in 1972, but failed to be ratified by the states.[8] It has been reintroduced nearly every year since 1982,[9] most recently in 2011 by Rep. Carolyn Maloney and Sen. Robert Menendez.[10]

NOW activities are divided between NOW and the National Organization for Women Foundation (NOW Foundation). The former is a 501(c)(4) non-profit organization, which means that it is exempt from paying federal income tax (although donations to it are not tax-deductible) and it is allowed to spend unlimited funds on lobbying. The latter was founded by NOW in 1986 as a 501(c)(3) non-profit organization, which means that it is exempt from paying federal income tax (and donations to it are tax-deductible) although it is not allowed to lobby.[11]

NOW and the NOW Foundation have tremendous assets to expend on programs. As shown in figure 7-2, NOW had total revenue of over $3 million, most of which came from membership fees (these membership fees were turned over to the NOW Foundation).

NOW's and the NOW Foundation's expenditures on programs are detailed in table 7-2 and 7-3. As the tables show, NOW spent over 2 million dollars on its programs to promote awareness of women's issues and to advance women's rights, as well as to support local chapters with parallel activities, and the NOW Foundation spent over a half million dollars on its activities. No wonder NOW and the NOW Foundation are so successful at capturing the attention of lawmakers when they are able to spend so lavishly on their lobbying and programs. Unfortunately, there is no comparable lobbying organization for women who do not want special preferences for women.

FIGURE 7-2

National Organization for Women Revenue, 2009

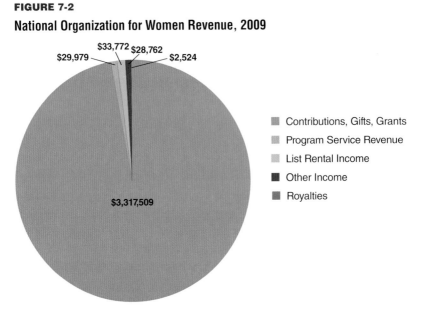

SOURCE: National Organization for Women, Inc., *U.S. Internal Revenue Service 2009 Form 990* (2010).

TABLE 7-2

National Organization for Women Expenses, 2009

Program Service Expenses		Management and General Expenses	Fundraising Expenses
Activity	Expense		
Education and awareness: promoting public awareness and education regarding issues impacting women's rights	$ 280,281		
Regions, states, and chapters: money utilized by local units for local projects to promote women's rights	$ 564,531		
General issues: support of issues promoting women's rights	$ 512,056		
Other program expenses: membership development, conference, development of legislative strategies for politics	$ 706,214		
TOTAL:	$2,063,082	$284,564	$252,664

SOURCE: National Organization for Women, Inc., *U.S. Internal Revenue Service 2009 Form 990* (2010).

TABLE 7-3

National Organization for Women Foundation Expenses, 2009

Program Service Expenses		Management and General Expenses	Fundraising Expenses
Activity	Expense		
Education and awareness: promoting the understanding and consciousness of society regarding women's issues and equal rights and opportunities for all	$ 6,526		
General issues: conferences, litigations, advocacy, leadership training and other programs to advance women's rights	$517,954		
Other program expenses: money utilized by local units, communications, conference, membership development	$ 13,826		
TOTAL:	**$543,171**	**$11,956**	**$23,443**

SOURCE: National Organization for Women, Inc., *U.S. Internal Revenue Service 2009 Form 990* (2010).

The American Association of University Women

The American Association of University Women, founded in 1881,[12] is a feminist organization of over 100,000 members and donors, 100 local branches, and 500 campus affiliates.[13] The AAUW is concerned with "gender equity" and puts significant emphasis on researching issues "such as the pay gap between men and women, economic security of older women, sexual harassment on college campuses, and gender equity in science and engineering education."[14] The AAUW claims that women earn on average 77 cents for every $1 that men earn and that there are various "environmental and social barriers—including stereotypes, gender bias and the climate of science and engineering departments in colleges and universities—that continue to block women's participation and progress in science, technology, engineering, and math."[15]

In making these statements, however, AAUW fails to acknowledge the difference in labor decisions and workplace experience that account for much of the gender gap, as well as explanations other than gender bias that help explain why relatively few women compared to men enter science, technology, engineering, and mathematics (STEM) programs and careers. As a result, AAUW supports policies such as affirmative action and the extension of Title IX to education.[16] In the legislative realm, AAUW is an ardent proponent of the Equal Rights Amendment and legislation to establish pay equity.[17]

Like NOW, AAUW includes a 501(c)(3) non-profit organization and a 501(c)(4) called the AAUW Educational Foundation and the AAUW Action Fund, respectively.[18] Both the AAUW Educational Foundation and the AAUW Action Fund have substantial net assets to advance the AAUW's agenda: in 2009, the AAUW Educational Foundation had over $13 million dollars, while the AAUW Action Fund had over $2 million in net assets. The AAUW Educational

FIGURE 7-3

American Association of University Women Educational Foundation Revenue, 2009

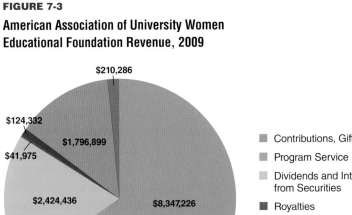

SOURCE: American Association of University Women, *U.S. Internal Revenue Service 2009 Form 990* (2010).

Foundation, which is able to accept tax-deductible gifts, received over $8 million in contributions, gifts, and grants. The AAUW Action Fund, which is not able to receive tax-deductible contributions, earned most of its revenue from membership dues.[19]

The AAUW Educational Foundation, which has considerably more funds than the smaller AAUW Action Fund, spent over $10 million to fund program service expenses and to advance its agenda in the fiscal year 2009, as shown in table 7-4. While the AAUW is concerned that women in general are underpaid, it compensated its top management lavishly: even before counting benefits, its Executive Director received $241,647, and the Chief Strategy Officer, the Director of Informational Technology, and the Director of Public Policy received $194,630, $151,089, and $169,501 respectively. The AAUW Action Fund, much smaller than the AAUW Education Foundation, spent nearly its entire budget of just under $1 million on membership services, as shown in table 7-5.

FIGURE 7-4

American Association of University Women Action Fund Revenue, 2009

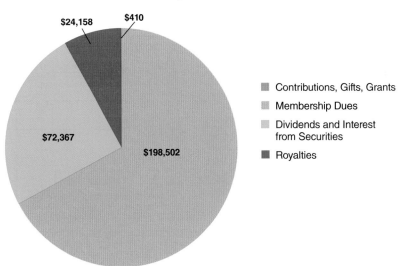

SOURCE: American Association of University Women, *U.S. Internal Revenue Service 2009 Form 990* (2010).

TABLE 7-4

AAUW Educational Foundation Expenses, 2009

Program Service Expenses		Management and General Expenses	Fundraising Expenses
Activity	**Expense**		
Outreach: Member recruitment and retention	$ 3,548,506		
American fellowships: fellowships awarded to women doing doctoral or post-doctoral work in the sciences, social sciences, arts, or humanities, with preference given to women in fields where women's participation has traditionally been low	$ 2,040,261		
Research and project grants: career development and community action grants	$ 1,300,254		
Other program expenses: professional meetings meetings and conferences, the Legal Advocacy Fund, publications, and the online directory of fellowship and grant recipients	$ 3,452,053		
TOTAL:	**$10,341,074**	**$1,343,264**	**$1,371,893**

NOTE: Fiscal year ending June 30, 2010.

SOURCE: American Association of University Women, *U.S. Internal Revenue Service 2009 Form 990* (2010).

TABLE 7-5

AAUW Action Fund Expenses, 2009

Program Service Expenses		Management and General Expenses	Fundraising Expenses
Activity	**Expense**		
Membership services: conducting recruitment and retention efforts	$941,456		
Advocacy: develops and implements effective legislative, regulatory, grassroots engagement and voter education strategies to advance AAUW's mission	$ 29,178		
TOTAL:	**$970,634**	**$25,893**	**$12,480**

SOURCE: American Association of University Women, *U.S. Internal Revenue Service 2009 Form 990* (2010).

National Women's Law Center

The National Women's Law Center is a nonprofit organization founded in 1972 that works to promote women's rights through "the law in all its forms: getting new laws on the books and enforced; litigating ground-breaking cases in state and federal courts all the way to the Supreme Court; and educating the public about ways to make the law and public policies work for women and their families."[20]

The NWLC is concerned with child care and early education, poverty and income support, gender equity in education, workplace fairness and flexibility, comprehensive and affordable health care, reproductive choices, judges and the courts, retirement security, and tax and budget priorities.[21] The NWLC works for equality for women in education and in the workplace. This is a misguided goal: while justice and fairness certainly call for guaranteeing all citizens equal access to education and jobs, this is entirely different from guaranteeing them equity.

The NWLC decries "the significant under-representation that young women face in too many fields."[22] This ignores women's gains in higher education and the data, discussed in chapter 2, that show that women receive well over half of all associate's, bachelor's, and master's degrees, and around half of all first professional and doctoral degrees. Moreover, if women on average continue to be more likely to study biology while men continue to be more likely to study physics, this is more likely a reflection of different aggregate preferences and abilities rather than rampant discrimination. The NWLC's lobbying for an expanded application of Title IX to ensure gender equity in fields of study and careers where women are under-represented is thus unnecessary.

Imposing gender equity on every field of study and every career is a preposterous goal which would amount to equal numbers of men and women to major in every field from comparative literature, to biology, to philosophy, to engineering. Men and women should be granted the freedom to choose what field to study and what career to pursue.

FIGURE 7-5

National Women's Law Center Revenue, 2009

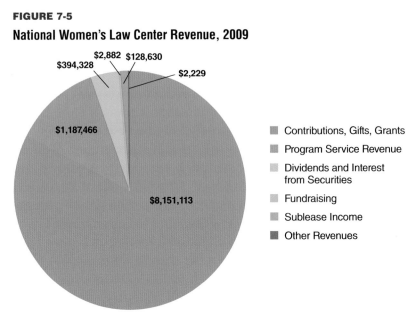

$394,328 $2,882 $128,630
                          $2,229

$1,187,466

$8,151,113

- Contributions, Gifts, Grants
- Program Service Revenue
- Dividends and Interest from Securities
- Fundraising
- Sublease Income
- Other Revenues

NOTE: Fiscal year ending June 30, 2009.

SOURCE: National Women's Law Center, *U.S. Internal Revenue Service 2009 Form 990* (2010).

Further, the NWLC asserts that "girls today represent only 15 percent of students taking classes in traditionally male, and higher-paid, fields such as carpentry, masonry and welding" and that "maids and housecleaners, for example, 87 percent of whom are female, make about $3,000 less each year than janitors and building cleaners, who are 72 percent male."[23] The NWLC believes this indicates that America is plagued by gender discrimination. However, as discussed in chapter 1, the relatively unpleasant and dangerous work conditions that in fields such as carpentry, masonry, welding, and janitorial services offer workers higher pay. Being a maid or a housecleaner is generally easier and more pleasant than being a janitor or building cleaner, and this degree of relative ease explains the pay gap. The fact that men tend to choose higher paid but more dangerous and less pleasant jobs than women likely indicates different preferences rather than discrimination that traps women in a "pink ghetto."

Like the other women's organizations discussed in this chapter, the NWLC has significant assets to support its programs. As of 2009,

TABLE 7-6

National Women's Law Center Expenses, 2009

Program Service Expenses		Management and General Expenses	Fundraising Expenses
Activity	Expense		
Health and reproductive rights: litigation, research, technical assistance, and public education efforts	$3,124,222		
Family economic security: litigation, research, technical assistance, and public education efforts	$1,888,053		
Women's legal rights: litigation, research, technical assistance, and public education efforts	$1,076,094		
Other program service expenses	$ 835,845		
TOTAL:	**$6,922,214**	**$806,506**	**$576,545**

NOTE: Fiscal year ending June 30, 2010.

SOURCE: National Women's Law Center, *U.S. Internal Revenue Service 2009 Form 990* (2010).

it had assets of over $25 million.[24] As shown in figure 7-5, the NWLC had total revenue of over $9 million, mostly gained from direct contributions, gifts, and grants.

As shown in table 7-6, the NWLC had total expenses of over $8 million, about five-sixths of which were spent on program service expenses in its 2009 fiscal year. Of these expenses, compensation for employees was the greatest part: the NWLC spent $1,066,581 (or 12 percent of its total expenses) on compensation for officers, directors, and key employees, as well as $3,558,766 (or 43 percent of its total expenses) on salaries and wages for other employees. The organization's two co-presidents were paid $305,585, or around $340,000 including benefits, while its two vice presidents were paid salaries of $150,800 and $157,100.

Catalyst

Catalyst, founded in 1962, is an organization devoted to "working globally with businesses and professions to build inclusive workplaces and expand opportunities for women and business."[25] Catalyst has

FIGURE 7-6

Catalyst Revenue, 2009

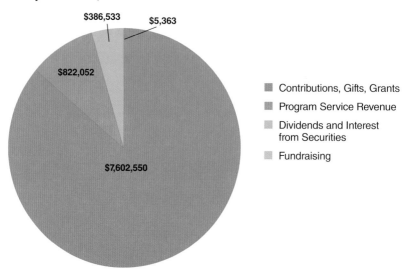

NOTE: Fiscal year ending August 31, 2009.

SOURCE: Catalyst, *U.S. Internal Revenue Service 2009 Form 990* (2010).

more than 400 member businesses and offices not only in the United States but also in Canada and Europe.[26]

Catalyst focuses on women in business and in the workplace, especially in the private sector. The organization conducts extensive research on women in leadership, organizational change and effectiveness, and diversity and inclusion.[27] Much of the research Catalyst conducts and the data it collects is available to the public online in the form of research briefs and reports.[28]

Additionally, Catalyst offers its member businesses guides to practices that organizations have taken to become more inclusive of women in their workforce and guidebooks that help organizations measure the effectiveness of their diversity and inclusion efforts.[29] One example of these resources is the Catalyst Gender Stereotype Risk Assessment Toolkit (SRAT), released in 2009, which allows "users to assess for the risk of gender stereotyping in corporate business units."[30] Catalyst also provides advice and consulting services to help

TABLE 7-7

Catalyst Expenses, 2009

Program Service Expenses		Management and General Expenses	Fundraising Expenses
Activity	Expense		
Communications: creates and executes strategies to increase Catalyst's visibility in the United States, Canada, and Europe	$2,135,365		
Research: conducts research on women's leadership advancement and work/ life issues; publication of studies and company best practices and recommendations for companies and firms	$2,023,948		
Information center and services: maintaining the Information Center, a clearinghouse of information on women and the workplace for staff, the media, the general public, and corporate contributors	$1,085,193		
Other program service expenses	$1,598,368		
TOTAL:	**$6,842,874**	**$1,187,150**	**$849,810**

NOTE: Fiscal year ending August 31, 2010.

SOURCE: Catalyst, *U.S. Internal Revenue Service 2009 Form 990* (2010).

its members improve workplace inclusion; and it collects data on gender diversity across companies and then allows members to view the aggregated and analyzed statistics so that companies will have a benchmark against which to measure the diversity of their workforce.[31]

Like the other organizations discussed in this chapter, Catalyst has substantial wealth to advance its agenda: it had over $14 million in assets at the end of fiscal year 2009.[32] That year, as shown in figure 7-6, Catalyst had revenue of $9 million, of which about 86 percent was received in the form of direct public support through contributions, gifts, and grants.

As shown in table 7-7, in the same year the organization also had total expenses of over $8 million, of which about three-quarters went to program service expenses. Nearly one-fith of its expenses were for compensation for officers, directors, and key employees and 44 percent of its total expenses were for salaries and wages for other employees.[33]

NOTES

1. National Organization for Women, "Frequently Asked Questions," http://www. now.org/organization/faq.html (accessed July 29, 2010).

2. Ibid.

3. Ibid.

4. National Organization for Women, "NOW and Economic Justice," http://www. now.org/issues/economic/index.html (accessed July 29, 2010).

5. Ibid.

6. National Organization for Women, "NOW and Constitutional Equality," http:// www.now.org/issues/constitution/index.html (accessed July 29, 2010).

7. National Organization for Women, "2009 National NOW Conference Resolutions," http://www.now.org/organization/conference/resolutions/2009.html (accessed July 29, 2010).

8. National Organization for Women, "Chronology of the Equal Rights Amendment, 1923–1996," http://www.now.org/issues/economic/cea/history.html (accessed July 29, 2010).

9. Roberta W. Francis, "Frequently Asked Questions," The Equal Rights Amendment, http://www.equalrightsamendment.org/faq.htm (accessed July 29, 2010).

10. "Rep. Maloney, Sen. Menendez reintroduce Equal Rights Amendment." Press Release June 22, 2011. http://maloney.house.gov/index.php?option=content&task =view&id=2380&Itemid=61(accessed September 26, 2011.)

11. National Organization for Women, "Highlights from NOW's Forty Fearless Years," http://www.now.org/history/timeline.html (accessed July 29, 2010).

12. American Association of University Women, "About AAUW," http://www.aauw. org/about/ (accessed August 3, 2010).

13. American Association of University Women, "AAUW's Organizational Structure," 29 July 2010 <http://www.aauw.org/about/aauw.cfm (accessed July 29, 2010).

14. American Association of University Women, "AAUW Research," http://www. aauw.org/learn/research/ (accessed July 30, 2010).

15. American Association of University Women, "Current Research Reports," Women, http://www.aauw.org/learn/research/current.cfm (accessed July 30, 2010).

16. American Association of University Women, "Principles and Priorities," http://www.aauw.org/act/issue_advocacy/principles_priorities.cfm (accessed July 30, 2010).

17. Ibid.

18. Ibid.

19. American Association of University Women, U.S. Internal Revenue Service 2009 Form 990, 2010.

20. National Women's Law Center, "About the National Women's Law Center," http://www.nwlc.org/display.cfm?section=About%20NWLC (accessed August 2, 2010).

21. Ibid.

22. National Women's Law Center, "A Platform For Progress: Building a Better Future for Women and Their Families," 2008, http://www.nwlc.org/pdf/Platform forProgress2008.pdf (accessed August 2, 2010).

23. Ibid.

24. National Women's Law Center, U.S. Internal Revenue Service 2009 Form 990, 2010.

25. Catalyst, *Catalyst Annual Report 2009*, 2009, http://www.catalyst.org/etc/annual-reports/CATALYST_Annual_Report_2009-web.pdf.

26. Ibid.

27. Catalyst, "Research and Knowledge," http://www.catalyst.org/page/52/research-knowledge (accessed August 2, 2010).

28. Catalyst, "Types of Research and Knowledge," http://www.catalyst.org/page/99/research-and-knowledge-types (accessed August 2, 2010).

29. Ibid.

30. Catalyst, "Gender Stereotype Risk Assessment Toolkit (SRAT)," http://www.catalyst.org/publication/354/catalyst-gender-stereotype-risk-assessment-toolkit-srat (accessed August 2, 2010).

31. Catalyst, "Catalyst Member Benchmarking," http://www.catalyst.org/page/296/catalyst-member-benchmarking (accessed August 2, 2010).

32. Catalyst, U.S. Internal Revenue Service 2009 Form 990, 2010.

33. Ibid.

PART
VIII

Conclusions

*E*very year, usually in April, members of Congress hold hearings on pay differences between men and women. The occasion is Equal Pay Day—the day of the year, according to feminists, when all women's wages, allegedly only 78 percent of all men's in 2011, "catch up" to what men have earned the year before. The story is that women need to work those extra months to achieve what men had achieved by New Year's.

On this occasion in 2011, President Obama stated, "When the Equal Pay Act was signed into law in 1963, women earned 59 cents for every dollar earned by men. Though women today are more likely than men to attend and graduate from college, women still earn an average of only about 77 cents for every dollar a man earns. Even when accounting for factors such as experience, education, industry, and hours, this wage gap persists. Over the course of her lifetime, this gap will cost a woman and her family lost wages, reduced pensions, and diminished Social Security benefits. Though we have made great strides, wage discrimination is real and women are still more likely to live in poverty. These inequities remind us to work even harder to close the gaps that still exist."[1]

The President is mistaken. Studies show that when women work at the same jobs as men, with the same accumulated lifetime work experience, they earn essentially the same salary.

But the myths of the pay gap, the mother's penalty, the glass ceiling, and the pink ghetto are leading the White House and Congress toward policies that favor women, already better-educated, at the expense of men. In particular, President Obama seeks to expand so-called gender parity under Title IX federal law beyond college athletics to college programs in science, technology, engineering, and mathematics (STEM); to promote parity in employment through the implementation of the Dodd-Frank financial regulations; and to expand access to services for women's health issues even while neglecting men's health initiatives. These policies would undermine America's meritocracy and cast doubt on women's legitimate achievements.

The Obama administration's misguided effort to extend Title IX gender-equity requirements from college sports to college STEM programs was discussed extensively in chapter 2. This effort does not take into account the evidence that women and men have different aptitudes and interests that cannot be overturned by federal policy. Meanwhile, the administration does not appear to be concerned about whether men are deprived of taking literature, music, art, psychology, and biology by larger numbers of female majors. (They are not, just as women are not deprived of taking STEM classes.) If Title IX is going to be extended to academic subjects, why stop at math and science?

Many of the most admired and successful women in America—such as Secretaries of State Hillary Clinton and Condoleezza Rice, cable television show host Oprah Winfrey, Ebay founder Meg Whitman—did not get degrees from STEM programs. Two world leaders, former British Prime Minister Margaret Thatcher and Germany's Chancellor Angela Merkel, did get degrees in STEM, but rose to political power after leaving their science careers behind.

The Obama administration is also trying to promote parity in employment in fields where women have been supposedly underrepresented. One of President Obama's signature pieces of legislation, the Dodd-Frank financial regulation bill, requires race and gender employment ratios to be observed by private financial institutions that do business with the government. In a dramatic departure from current employment law, "fair inclusion" provisions for women and minorities (which are likely to lead to de facto quotas) have been imposed on America's financial industry.

The Dodd-Frank legislation will establish not only more than a dozen new financial regulatory offices but almost 30 Offices of Minority and Women Inclusion. In a senseless expansion of the federal bureaucracy, these offices will develop policies promoting equal employment opportunities and racial, ethnic, and gender diversity of not just the agency's workforce, but also the workforces of its contractors and subcontractors. This means that not only must financial institutions demonstrate that they have a diverse workforce, but also the firms with whom the agency contracts to shred its documents, to clean its offices, and to cater office parties must demonstrate "fair inclusion" of women and minorities. If an agency director decides that a contractor has not made a good-faith effort to include women and minorities in its workforce, he or she is required to contact the agency administrator and recommend that the contract be terminated. Even if no women apply, "fair inclusion" is still the law of the land. The law's language compels agencies to search for underrepresented groups at women's colleges, job fairs, girls' high schools, and through advertising in women's magazines.

This latest attempt by Congress to dictate what "fair" employment means is likely to encourage government and private sector managers to hire women and minorities for the sake of appearances, even if some new hires are less qualified than other applicants. The result is likely to be redundant hiring and a wasteful expansion of payroll overhead. Moreover, employers may find it easier to employ and contract with less-qualified women and minorities, merely in order to avoid regulatory trouble. This would hurt women and make them second-class citizens in the workplace.

Finally, although women live an average of five years longer than men, the Obama administration expanded access to women's health services without similarly expanding access to men's health services. The Patient Protection and Affordable Care Act mentions seven offices and coordinating committees especially for women but not one for men; the word "breast" is mentioned 42 times in the Act but the word "prostate" not even once.

The new law creates full employment for professionals specializing in women's health: the Act names three Offices of Women's Health within the Department of Health and Human Services, a Coordinating Committee on Women's Health (with senior representatives from each of the Department's agencies and offices), a National Women's Information Center to facilitate information exchange as well as "coordinate efforts to promote women's health programs and policies with the private sector," and an Office of Women's Health in both the Food and Drug Administration and the Centers for Disease Control and Prevention. These seven offices are charged with promoting women's health and identifying women's health projects deserving of federal funding. The budgets in the new offices created by the new law appear to be unlimited—the statute simply says that "there are authorized to be appropriated *such sums as may be necessary* [italics added] for each of the fiscal years 2010 through 2014."

Not only is the federal government overtly favoring women's health over men's, but provisions in the reform bill ensure that the government will provide incentives for the private sector to do the same through the National Women's Health Information Service and the Office of Women's Health. The Secretary of Health and Human Services will also be empowered to enter into contracts with and make grants to "public and private entities, agencies and organizations" to enable the Office of Women's Health to carry out its activities. These provisions will encourage researchers and hospitals to neglect men's health in favor of women's in order to contract with and receive grants from the federal government.

Many people might ask: who would set up multiple government bureaucracies and spend untold billions of dollars to help women who are already more highly educated than men? Or distort hiring practices in a way that will impose great costs on government and businesses without clearly benefiting women? Or to advance women's health, but not men's, when women already live longer than men?

The answer, sadly, is that feminists, and the politicians who do their bidding, seek to rebuild America according to their own distorted views according to which women are perpetual victims and in perpetual need of government assistance. These feminists and politicians make their careers by telling women that they are defeated. No Washington government official bothers to hail the victory of women in everyday America. Instead, they tell America that women need government help. They tell America that Washington has the answer: more laws and more regulations designed to give women additional advantages at the expense of men.

The distorted America would not matter if the federal government were unimportant in our economy and our society. But Washington makes sure that it is important. It makes sure that all aspects of everyday America—the America in which women are triumphant—are put under the thumb of some Washington bureaucrat.

The message that women are weak victims contradicts the views of the original feminists who fought for the right to vote, the right to work while pregnant and with small children, and the right to equal wages for the same work. Fifty years ago it was permitted to advertise jobs with one salary for men and another for women. Times have changed, and now not only are such practices illegal but culturally unacceptable.

Many feminists, however, imagine that employers treat women as less valuable than men. These activists argue, contrary to overwhelming evidence, that women can only succeed with government assistance—in math and science, in financial industry employment, and in healthcare. Anti-discrimination laws are not sufficient, they say, and they call for quotas. A woman's choice of less time at the office and more time at home with family is not considered an opportunity but a social problem calling for a government solution.

Women face conflicting accounts of women's status in America. On the one hand, they succeed in their daily lives. On the other hand, they have the federal government belittling them, telling them that they are defeated, that they are victims, that their efforts are hopeless, that they cannot succeed.

Meanwhile, the federal government wants to steal women's earned success and ascribe it to official intervention. It wants to brand women as losers in search of help, with the federal government being the brave knight to rescue the damsels in distress. American women, so Americans are told, cannot succeed on their own. They need the protection of the federal government in every aspect of their lives.

It is time for American women to stand up. Government programs that attempt to guarantee outcomes favorable to women undermine the achievements and choices that women make every day without such programs. Such programs do not help women; they harm women. Like all Americans, women succeed not because the federal government guarantees their success but precisely because it does not.

NOTES

1. President Obama, "National Equal Pay Day, 2011," April 11, 2011 White House press release, http://www.dol.gov/wb/equal-pay/2011-Equal-Pay-Day-Proclamation.pdf (accessed September 12, 2011).

APPENDIX

Statistical Tables

*T*his appendix presents tables that provide the data points for the figures in chapters 1–7. The table numbers correspond to the figure numbers.

TABLE A1-1:

Percentage of Women Who Work, 1970–2011

Year		Year		Year		Year	
1970	43.3%	1980	51.5%	1990	57.5%	2000	59.9%
1971	43.4%	1981	52.1%	1991	57.4%	2001	59.8%
1972	43.9%	1982	52.6%	1992	57.8%	2002	59.6%
1973	44.7%	1983	52.9%	1993	57.9%	2003	59.5%
1974	45.7%	1984	53.6%	1994	58.8%	2004	59.2%
1975	46.3%	1985	54.5%	1995	58.9%	2005	59.3%
1976	47.3%	1986	55.3%	1996	59.3%	2006	59.4%
1977	48.4%	1987	56.0%	1997	59.8%	2007	59.3%
1978	50.0%	1988	56.6%	1998	59.8%	2008	59.5%
1979	50.9%	1989	57.4%	1999	60.0%	2009	59.2%
						2010	58.6%
						2011	58.3%

SOURCE: U.S. Department of Labor, Bureau of Labor Statistics, Current Population Survey.

TABLE A1-2:

Women's Share of the Labor Force, 1970–2011

Year		Year		Year		Year	
1970	38.1%	1980	42.5%	1990	45.2%	2000	46.5%
1971	38.2%	1981	43.0%	1991	45.3%	2001	46.5%
1972	38.5%	1982	43.3%	1992	45.4%	2002	46.5%
1973	38.9%	1983	43.5%	1993	45.5%	2003	46.6%
1974	39.4%	1984	43.8%	1994	46.0%	2004	46.4%
1975	40.0%	1985	44.2%	1995	46.1%	2005	46.4%
1976	40.5%	1986	44.5%	1996	46.2%	2006	46.3%
1977	41.0%	1987	44.8%	1997	46.2%	2007	46.4%
1978	41.7%	1988	45.0%	1998	46.3%	2008	46.5%
1979	42.1%	1989	45.2%	1999	46.5%	2009	46.7%
						2010	46.7%
						2011	46.7%

SOURCE: U.S. Department of Labor, Bureau of Labor Statistics, Current Population Survey.

TABLE A1-3:

Total Employment by Sex, 1970–2011 (thousands of workers)

Year	Men	Women	Year	Men	Women	Year	Men	Women
1970	48,990	29,688	1984	59,091	45,915	1998	70,693	60,771
1971	49,391	29,976	1985	59,891	47,259	1999	71,446	62,042
1972	50,896	31,257	1986	60,892	48,706	2000	73,305	63,586
1973	52,349	32,715	1987	62,107	50,334	2001	73,196	63,737
1974	53,025	33,770	1988	63,273	51,696	2002	72,903	63,582
1975	51,858	33,989	1989	64,306	53,020	2003	73,332	64,404
1976	53,138	35,615	1990	65,104	53,689	2004	74,524	64,728
1977	54,729	37,289	1991	64,223	53,496	2005	75,973	65,757
1978	56,480	39,569	1992	64,440	54,052	2006	77,502	66,925
1979	57,608	41,218	1993	65,349	54,910	2007	78,254	67,792
1980	57,186	42,117	1994	66,449	56,616	2008	77,486	67,876
1981	57,397	43,000	1995	67,377	57,523	2009	73,670	66,208
1982	56,271	43,256	1996	68,207	58,501	2010	73,358	65,710
1983	56,787	44,047	1997	69,685	59,873	2011	73,961	65,487

SOURCE: U.S. Department of Labor, Bureau of Labor Statistics, Current Population Survey.

TABLE A1-4:

Full-Time Employment by Sex, 1970–2011 (thousands of workers)

Year	Men	Women	Year	Men	Women	Year	Men	Women
1970	44,825	21,929	1984	53,070	33,473	1998	63,189	45,014
1971	45,023	21,950	1985	53,862	34,672	1999	63,930	46,372
1972	46,373	22,842	1986	54,685	35,845	2000	65,930	47,916
1973	47,843	23,960	1987	55,746	37,210	2001	65,623	47,950
1974	48,378	24,714	1988	56,816	38,398	2002	65,205	47,494
1975	46,988	24,598	1989	57,885	39,484	2003	65,379	47,946
1976	48,150	25,814	1990	58,501	40,165	2004	66,444	48,073
1977	49,551	27,076	1991	57,407	39,783	2005	67,858	49,158
1978	51,281	28,912	1992	57,363	40,301	2006	69,307	50,380
1979	52,427	30,227	1993	58,123	40,991	2007	70,035	51,056
1980	51,717	30,845	1994	58,832	40,940	2008	68,853	51,178
1981	51,906	31,337	1995	59,936	41,743	2009	63,951	48,683
1982	50,334	31,086	1996	60,762	42,776	2010	63,494	48,215
1983	50,643	31,679	1997	62,258	44,076	2011	64,170	49,003

SOURCE: U.S. Department of Labor, Bureau of Labor Statistics, Current Population Survey.

TABLE A1-5:

Part-Time Employment by Sex, 1970–2011 (thousands of workers)

Year	Men	Women	Year	Men	Women	Year	Men	Women
1970	4,166	7,758	1984	6,020	12,441	1998	7,504	15,757
1971	4,367	8,026	1985	6,028	12,587	1999	7,516	15,670
1972	4,523	8,416	1986	6,207	12,862	2000	7,375	15,670
1973	4,507	8,756	1987	6,360	13,124	2001	7,573	15,788
1974	4,646	9,055	1988	6,457	13,298	2002	7,697	16,088
1975	4,870	9,391	1989	6,430	13,544	2003	7,953	16,459
1976	4,988	9,799	1990	6,604	13,524	2004	8,080	16,654
1977	5,178	10,213	1991	6,815	13,713	2005	8,115	16,598
1978	5,198	10,658	1992	7,077	13,751	2006	8,194	16,545
1979	5,180	10,990	1993	7,226	13,919	2007	8,220	16,736
1980	5,471	11,270	1994	7,617	15,670	2008	8,634	16,698
1981	5,492	11,664	1995	7,441	15,779	2009	9,719	17,525
1982	5,937	12,170	1996	7,445	15,725	2010	9,858	17,493
1983	6,145	12,367	1997	7,427	15,797	2011	9,872	17,055

SOURCE: U.S. Department of Labor, Bureau of Labor Statistics, Current Population Survey.

TABLE A1-6:

Women's Labor Force Participation Rates by Marital Status, 1970–2011

Year	Single (never married)	Married (spouse present)	Year	Single (never married)	Married (spouse present)
1970	56.8%	40.5%	1990	66.7%	58.4%
1971	56.4%	40.6%	1991	66.2%	58.5%
1972	57.5%	41.2%	1992	66.2%	59.3%
1973	58.6%	42.3%	1993	66.2%	59.4%
1974	59.5%	43.3%	1994	66.7%	60.7%
1975	59.8%	44.3%	1995	66.8%	61.0%
1976	61.0%	45.3%	1996	67.1%	61.2%
1977	62.1%	46.4%	1997	67.9%	61.6%
1978	63.7%	47.8%	1998	68.5%	61.2%
1979	64.6%	49.0%	1999	68.7%	61.2%
1980	64.4%	49.8%	2000	68.9%	61.1%
1981	64.5%	50.5%	2001	68.1%	61.2%
1982	65.1%	51.1%	2002	67.4%	61.0%
1983	65.0%	51.8%	2003	66.2%	61.0%
1984	65.6%	52.8%	2004	65.9%	60.5%
1985	66.6%	53.8%	2005	66.0%	60.7%
1986	67.2%	54.9%	2006	65.7%	61.0%
1987	67.4%	55.9%	2007	65.3%	61.0%
1988	67.7%	56.7%	2008	65.3%	61.4%
1989	68.0%	57.8%	2009	64.2%	61.4%
			2010	63.2%	60.9%
			2011	61.9%	60.6%

SOURCE: U.S. Department of Labor, Bureau of Labor Statistics, Current Population Survey.

TABLE A1-7:

Unemployment Rates by Sex, 1970–2011

Year	Men	Women	Year	Men	Women	Year	Men	Women
1970	4.4%	5.9%	1984	7.4%	7.6%	1998	4.4%	4.6%
1971	5.3%	6.9%	1985	7.0%	7.4%	1999	4.1%	4.3%
1972	4.9%	6.6%	1986	6.9%	7.1%	2000	3.9%	4.1%
1973	4.1%	6.0%	1987	6.2%	6.2%	2001	4.8%	4.7%
1974	4.8%	6.7%	1988	5.5%	5.6%	2002	5.9%	5.6%
1975	7.9%	9.3%	1989	5.2%	5.4%	2003	6.3%	5.7%
1976	7.0%	8.6%	1990	5.7%	5.5%	2004	5.6%	5.4%
1977	6.2%	8.2%	1991	7.2%	6.4%	2005	5.1%	5.1%
1978	5.2%	7.2%	1992	7.9%	7.0%	2006	4.6%	4.6%
1979	5.1%	6.8%	1993	7.2%	6.6%	2007	4.7%	4.5%
1980	6.9%	7.4%	1994	6.2%	6.0%	2008	6.1%	5.4%
1981	7.4%	7.9%	1995	5.6%	5.6%	2009	10.4%	8.1%
1982	9.9%	9.4%	1996	5.4%	5.4%	2010	10.5%	8.6%
1983	9.9%	9.2%	1997	4.9%	5.0%	2011	10.4%	8.5%

SOURCE: U.S. Department of Labor, Bureau of Labor Statistics, Current Population Survey.

TABLE A1-8:

Distribution of Women's Labor Force (25 to 64 years) by Educational Attainment, 1970–2010

Year	< High School	High School Graduate	1-3 Years College	4+ Years College
1970	33.5	44.3	10.9	11.2
1971	32.2	44.2	11.9	11.8
1972	30.7	45.1	11.8	12.4
1973	28.4	45.9	12.4	13.3
1974	26.7	45.3	13.4	14.6
1975	26.5	45.5	13.9	14.1
1976	24.0	45.1	14.7	16.2
1977	22.8	45.1	15.2	16.9
1978	22.0	44.9	16.1	17.0
1979	20.1	45.0	17.1	17.8
1980	18.4	45.4	17.4	18.7
1981	17.4	46.1	17.9	18.6
1982	16.6	45.6	18.3	19.5
1983	15.6	44.8	18.8	20.9
1984	14.5	44.9	18.9	21.7
1985	13.7	44.4	19.9	22.0
1986	13.2	44.3	20.3	22.2
1987	12.5	44.0	20.7	22.8
1988	12.4	43.3	21.2	23.1
1989	11.9	42.9	20.9	24.3
1990	11.3	42.4	21.9	24.5
1991	10.9	41.6	22.2	25.2
1992	10.3	37.4	27.3	25.0
1993	9.3	36.6	28.4	25.7
1994	9.0	35.0	29.8	26.2
1995	8.8	34.1	30.2	26.9
1996	8.8	33.6	29.9	27.8
1997	8.7	33.5	29.4	28.4
1998	8.8	32.7	29.4	29.2
1999	8.5	32.1	29.5	29.9
2000	8.5	31.6	29.8	30.1
2001	8.4	31.0	30.2	30.4
2002	8.1	30.6	29.9	31.3
2003	7.9	30.0	29.9	32.2
2004	7.7	29.4	30.2	32.6
2005	7.7	28.7	30.2	33.3
2006	7.6	28.3	30.2	33.9
2007	7.1	27.9	30.1	34.9
2008	6.9	27.2	30.4	35.6
2009	7.0	26.7	30.3	36.0
2010	8.6	26.8	31.7	33.0

SOURCE: U.S. Department of Labor, Bureau of Labor Statistics, *Women in the Labor Force: A Databook* (2010), table 9.

TABLE A1-9:

Women's Median Usual Weekly Earnings as a Percentage of Men's, 1979–2011

Year	Percent	Year	Percent	Year	Percent	Year	Percent
1979	62.3	1987	69.8	1995	75.5	2003	79.4
1980	64.2	1988	70.2	1996	75.0	2004	80.4
1981	64.4	1989	70.1	1997	74.4	2005	81.1
1982	65.7	1990	71.9	1998	76.3	2006	80.8
1983	66.5	1991	74.2	1999	76.5	2007	80.2
1984	67.6	1992	75.8	2000	76.9	2008	79.8
1985	68.1	1993	77.1	2001	76.4	2009	80.1
1986	69.5	1994	76.4	2002	77.9	2010	81.2
						2011	82.4

SOURCE: U.S. Department of Labor, Bureau of Labor Statistics, *Women in the Labor Force: A Databook* (2010), table 16; *Employment and Earnings* (January 2010), annual averages, table 37.

TABLE A1-10:

Gender Wage Ratio by Presence and Age of Children, 2010
(All marital statuses included)

Characteristic	Female-Male Wage Ratio
Overall	81.2%
with children under 18 years old	72.5%
with children under 6 years old	75.6%
with no children under 18 years old	87.0%

SOURCE: U.S. Department of Labor, Bureau of Labor Statistics, *Highlights of Women's Earnings in 2009* (2010).

TABLE A1-11:

Women as a Percentage of Total Employment by Occupation, 1983, 1997, and 2010

Occupation	1983	1997	2010
Public Administration	36.2	49.5	45.0
Financial Managers	38.0	49.3	52.8
Accountant/Auditors	40.7	56.6	59.1
Insurance Underwriters	42.6	70.1	60.0
Health and Medicine Managers	60.7	76.8	72.1

SOURCE: U.S. Department of Labor, Bureau of Labor Statistics, *Employment and Earnings* (January 2010) unpublished tabulations from Current Population Survey.

TABLE A1-12:

Percentage Monthly Change in the Number of Jobs in Selected Sectors, December 2007–December 2010

Year	Construction	Service-providing	Year	Construction	Service-providing
2007–Dec	−0.64%	0.12%	2009–Jun	−22.6%	−3.3%
2008–Jan	−0.8%	0.2%	2009–Jul	−23.9%	−3.5%
2008–Feb	−1.4%	0.1%	2009–Aug	−25.2%	−3.6%
2008–Mar	−1.8%	0.1%	2009–Sep	−26.3%	−3.7%
2008–Apr	−2.7%	0.1%	2009–Oct	−27.3%	−3.8%
2008–May	−3.4%	−0.1%	2009–Dec	−28.6%	−3.8%
2008–Jun	−4.4%	−0.1%	2010–Jan	−29.7%	−3.8%
2008–Jul	−5.1%	−0.2%	2010–Feb	−30.7%	−3.8%
2008–Aug	−5.7%	−0.3%	2010–Mar	−30.4%	−3.6%
2008–Sep	−6.7%	−0.6%	2010–Apr	−30.1%	−3.4%
2008–Oct	−7.8%	−0.8%	2010–May	−30.7%	−3.0%
2008–Nov	−10.0%	−1.3%	2010–June	−31.1%	−3.2%
2008–Dec	−11.7%	−1.6%	2010–July	−31.3%	−3.3%
2009–Jan	−13.8%	−1.9%	2010–Aug	−30.9%	−3.3%
2009–Feb	−15.4%	−2.3%	2010–Sept	−31.0%	−3.3%
2009–Mar	−17.9%	−2.7%	2010–Oct	−31.0%	−3.2%
2009–Apr	−20.1%	−3.0%	2010–Nov	−31.2%	−3.1%
2009–May	−21.0%	−3.1%	2010–Dec	−31.3%	−3.0%

SOURCE: U.S. Department of Labor, Bureau of Labor Statistics, Establishment Survey.

TABLE A1-13:

Women in State Legislative Elections, 1992–2010

Election Year	Candidates	Winners and Holdovers
1992	2,302	1,460
1994	2,222	1,473
1996	2,215	1,528
1998	2,213	1,591
2000	2,228	1,656
2002	2,348	1,643
2004	2,220	1,664
2006	2,429	1,736
2008	2,337	1,786
2010	2,523	1,720

SOURCE: Center for American Women and Politics, Eagleton Institute of Politics, Rutgers University, *National Information Bank on Women in Public Office.*

TABLE A1-14:

Number of Women Candidates for U.S. Congressional Offices, 1970–2010

Year	Total	Year	Total	Year	Total	Year	Total
1970	26	1980	57	1990	77	2000	128
1972	34	1982	58	1992	117	2002	135
1974	47	1984	75	1994	121	2004	151
1976	55	1986	70	1996	129	2006	148
1978	48	1988	61	1998	131	2008	139
						2010	153

NOTES: Minor party candidates are included only if their parties have recently won statewide offices. Data since 1990 do not include the delegates from Washington D.C. and the five territories.

SOURCE: Center for American Women and Politics, Eagleton Institute of Politics, Rutgers University, *National Information Bank on Women in Public Office.*

TABLE A1-15:

Number of Women in U.S. Congress, 1971–2011

Year	Total	Year	Total	Year	Total	Year	Total
1971	15	1981	23	1991	32	2001	73
1973	16	1983	24	1993	54	2003	74
1975	19	1985	25	1995	57	2005	82
1977	20	1987	25	1997	63	2007	88
1979	17	1989	31	1999	65	2009	90
						2011	88

SOURCE: Center for American Women and Politics, Eagleton Institute of Politics, Rutgers University, *National Information Bank on Women in Public Office.*

TABLE A2-1:

Share of Degrees Earned by Women, 1970–2020*

Year	Associate	Bachelor's	Master's	First-professional	Doctoral
1970	43.0%	43.1%	39.7%	5.3%	13.3%
1971	42.9%	43.4%	40.1%	6.3%	14.3%
1972	43.1%	43.6%	40.6%	6.2%	15.8%
1973	44.5%	43.8%	41.3%	7.1%	17.8%
1974	45.2%	44.2%	43.0%	9.8%	19.1%
1975	47.0%	45.3%	44.8%	12.4%	21.3%
1976	46.4%	45.5%	46.4%	15.6%	22.9%
1977	48.1%	46.1%	47.1%	18.6%	24.3%
1978	50.3%	47.1%	48.3%	21.5%	26.4%
1979	52.3%	48.2%	49.1%	23.5%	28.1%
1980	54.2%	49.0%	49.4%	24.8%	29.7%
1981	54.7%	49.8%	50.3%	26.6%	31.1%
1982	54.7%	50.3%	50.8%	27.5%	32.1%
1983	54.6%	50.6%	50.1%	29.8%	33.2%
1984	55.2%	50.5%	49.5%	31.0%	33.6%
1985	55.4%	50.7%	49.9%	32.8%	34.1%
1986	56.0%	50.8%	50.3%	33.4%	35.2%
1987	56.3%	51.5%	51.2%	35.0%	35.2%
1988	56.3%	52.0%	51.5%	35.7%	35.1%
1989	57.3%	52.6%	51.9%	36.4%	36.6%
1990	58.0%	53.2%	52.6%	38.1%	36.4%
1991	58.8%	53.9%	53.6%	39.1%	37.0%
1992	58.9%	54.2%	54.1%	39.2%	37.1%
1993	58.8%	54.3%	54.2%	40.1%	38.1%
1994	59.4%	54.5%	54.5%	40.7%	38.5%
1995	59.5%	54.6%	55.1%	40.8%	39.4%
1996	60.5%	55.1%	55.9%	41.7%	39.9%
1997	60.8%	55.6%	56.9%	42.1%	40.8%
1998	61.0%	56.1%	57.1%	42.9%	42.0%
1999	61.0%	56.8%	57.7%	43.5%	42.9%
2000	60.2%	57.2%	58.0%	44.7%	44.1%
2001	60.0%	57.3%	58.5%	46.2%	44.9%
2002	60.0%	57.4%	58.7%	47.3%	46.3%
2003	60.0%	57.5%	58.8%	48.2%	47.1%
2004	60.9%	57.5%	58.9%	49.2%	47.7%
2005	61.6%	57.4%	59.3%	49.8%	48.8%
2006	62.1%	57.5%	60.0%	49.8%	48.9%
2007	62.2%	57.4%	60.6%	50.0%	50.1%
2008	62.3%	57.3%	60.6%	49.7%	51.0%
2009	62.1%	57.2%	60.4%	49.0%	52.3%
2010*	62.7%	57.0%	59.7%	49.6%	52.0%
2011*	63.0%	56.8%	59.2%	49.4%	52.6%
2012*	63.1%	56.6%	59.8%	49.1%	52.9%
2013*	63.3%	56.7%	60.1%	49.2%	53.4%
2014*	63.8%	56.9%	60.4%	49.4%	53.8%
2015*	64.0%	57.2%	60.4%	49.7%	54.1%
2016*	64.4%	57.3%	60.4%	50.1%	54.5%
2017*	64.7%	57.5%	60.4%	50.4%	54.8%
2018*	65.1%	57.7%	60.6%	50.6%	55.0%
2019*	65.3%	57.9%	60.7%	51.0%	55.4%
2020*	65.7%	58.0%	61.0%	51.3%	55.7%

* Projected

SOURCE: U.S. Department of Education, National Center for Education Statistics, *Digest of Education Statistics 2009* (2010).

TABLE A2-2:

Share of Bachelor's Degrees Awarded to Women, by Field of Study, 2008–2009

Fields of Study	Degrees Awarded to Women
Library sciences	89.7%
Family and consumer sciences/human sciences	87.4%
Health professions and related clinical sciences	85.2%
Education	79.2%
Legal professions and studies	72.9%
Liberal arts, general studies and humanities	64.7%
Communication and communications technologies	62.4%
Visual and performing arts	60.7%
Social sciences and history	49.4%
Business, management, and marketing	48.9%
Agriculture and natural resources	47.6%
Mathematics and statistics	43.3%
Physical sciences and science technologies	40.8%
Computer and information sciences	17.8%
Engineering and engineering technologies	16.5%

SOURCE: U.S. Department of Education, National Center for Education Statistics, *Digest of Education Statistics 2009* (2010).

TABLE A2-3:

Share of Master's Degrees in Business Awarded to Women, 1970–2009

Year		Year		Year		Year	
1970	3.6%	1980	22.3%	1990	34.0%	2000	39.9%
1971	3.9%	1981	25.0%	1991	35.0%	2001	40.8%
1972	3.9%	1982	27.8%	1992	35.4%	2002	41.1%
1973	4.9%	1983	29.0%	1993	35.7%	2003	41.1%
1974	6.5%	1984	30.2%	1994	36.5%	2004	42.0%
1975	8.4%	1985	31.0%	1995	37.0%	2005	42.4%
1976	11.6%	1986	31.1%	1996	37.6%	2006	42.9%
1977	14.3%	1987	33.1%	1997	39.0%	2007	44.0%
1978	16.8%	1988	33.6%	1998	38.7%	2008	44.6%
1979	19.1%	1989	33.6%	1999	39.8%	2009	45.3%

SOURCE: U.S. Department of Education, National Center for Education Statistics, *Digest of Education Statistics 2009* (2010).

TABLE A2-4:

Share of Law Degrees Awarded to Women, 1970–2009

Year		Year		Year		Year	
1970	5.4%	1980	30.2%	1990	42.2%	2000	45.9%
1971	7.1%	1981	32.4%	1991	43.0%	2001	47.3%
1972	6.9%	1982	33.4%	1992	42.7%	2002	48.0%
1973	8.0%	1983	36.1%	1993	42.5%	2003	49.0%
1974	11.4%	1984	36.8%	1994	43.0%	2004	49.4%
1975	15.1%	1985	38.5%	1995	42.6%	2005	48.7%
1976	19.2%	1986	39.0%	1996	43.5%	2006	48.0%
1977	22.5%	1987	40.2%	1997	43.7%	2007	47.6%
1978	26.0%	1988	40.5%	1998	44.4%	2008	47.0%
1979	28.5%	1989	40.9%	1999	44.8%	2009	45.8%

SOURCE: U.S. Department of Education, National Center for Education Statistics, *Digest of Education Statistics 2009* (2010).

TABLE A2-5:

Share of Dentistry Degrees Awarded to Women, 1970–2009

Year		Year		Year		Year	
1970	0.9%	1980	13.3%	1990	30.9%	2000	40.1%
1971	1.1%	1981	14.4%	1991	32.1%	2001	38.6%
1972	1.1%	1982	15.4%	1992	32.3%	2002	38.5%
1973	1.4%	1983	17.1%	1993	33.9%	2003	38.9%
1974	1.9%	1984	19.6%	1994	38.5%	2004	41.6%
1975	3.1%	1985	20.7%	1995	36.4%	2005	43.8%
1976	4.4%	1986	22.6%	1996	35.8%	2006	44.5%
1977	7.3%	1987	24.0%	1997	36.9%	2007	44.6%
1978	10.9%	1988	26.3%	1998	38.2%	2008	44.5%
1979	11.8%	1989	26.8%	1999	35.5%	2009	46.3%

SOURCE: U.S. Department of Education, National Center for Education Statistics, *Digest of Education Statistics 2009* (2010).

TABLE A2-6:

Share of Medical Degrees Awarded to Women, 1970–2009

Year		Year		Year		Year	
1970	8.4%	1980	23.4%	1990	34.2%	2000	42.7%
1971	9.1%	1981	24.7%	1991	36.0%	2001	43.3%
1972	9.0%	1982	25.0%	1992	35.7%	2002	44.4%
1973	8.9%	1983	26.7%	1993	37.7%	2003	45.3%
1974	11.1%	1984	28.2%	1994	37.9%	2004	46.4%
1975	13.1%	1985	30.4%	1995	38.8%	2005	47.3%
1976	16.2%	1986	30.8%	1996	40.9%	2006	48.9%
1977	19.1%	1987	32.4%	1997	41.4%	2007	49.2%
1978	21.5%	1988	33.1%	1998	41.6%	2008	49.3%
1979	23.0%	1989	33.3%	1999	42.5%	2009	48.9%

SOURCE: U.S. Department of Education, National Center for Education Statistics, *Digest of Education Statistics 2009* (2010).

TABLE A3-1:

Share of Population below the Poverty Line by Sex, 1970–2010

Year	Men	Women	Year	Men	Women	Year	Men	Women
1970	11.1%	14.0%	1984	12.8%	15.9%	1998	11.1%	14.3%
1971	10.8%	14.1%	1985	12.3%	15.6%	1999	10.4%	13.2%
1972	10.2%	13.4%	1986	11.8%	15.2%	2000	9.9%	12.6%
1973	9.6%	12.5%	1987	12.0%	15.0%	2001	10.4%	12.9%
1974	10.2%	12.9%	1988	11.5%	14.5%	2002	10.9%	13.3%
1975	10.7%	13.8%	1989	11.2%	14.4%	2003	11.2%	13.7%
1976	10.1%	13.4%	1990	11.7%	15.2%	2004	11.5%	13.9%
1977	10.0%	13.0%	1991	12.3%	16.0%	2005	11.1%	14.1%
1978	9.6%	13.0%	1992	12.9%	16.6%	2006	11.0%	13.6%
1979	10.0%	13.2%	1993	13.3%	16.9%	2007	11.1%	13.8%
1980	11.2%	14.7%	1994	12.8%	16.3%	2008	12.0%	14.4%
1981	12.1%	15.8%	1995	12.2%	15.4%	2009	13.0%	15.6%
1982	13.4%	16.5%	1996	12.0%	15.4%	2010	14.0%	16.2%
1983	13.5%	16.8%	1997	11.6%	14.9%			

SOURCE: U.S. Bureau of the Census, Current Population Survey, Annual Social and Economic Supplements.

TABLE A3-2:

Poverty Rate by Age and Sex, 2010

Age Group	Male	Female	Age Group	Male	Female
Under 5 years	26.5%	25.1%	45 to 54 years	9.6%	11.5%
5 to 17 years	20.5%	20.5%	55 to 59 years	9.5%	10.6%
18 to 24 years	18.8%	25.2%	60 to 64 years	9.3%	10.8%
25 to 34 years	12.5%	18.0%	65 to 74 years	6.5%	9.5%
35 to 44 years	11.1%	14.1%	75 years and over	7.0%	12.1%

SOURCE: U.S. Bureau of the Census, Current Population Survey, Annual Social and Economic Supplement.

TABLE A3-3:

Median Age at First Marriage by Sex, 1970–2010

Year	Men	Women	Year	Men	Women	Year	Men	Women
1970	23.2	20.8	1984	25.4	23.0	1998	26.7	25.0
1971	23.1	20.9	1985	25.5	23.3	1999	26.9	25.1
1972	23.3	20.9	1986	25.7	23.1	2000	26.8	25.1
1973	23.2	21.0	1987	25.8	23.6	2001	26.9	25.1
1974	23.1	21.1	1988	25.9	23.6	2002	26.9	25.3
1975	23.5	21.1	1989	26.2	23.8	2003	27.1	25.3
1976	23.8	21.3	1990	26.1	23.9	2004	27.4	25.3
1977	24.0	21.6	1991	26.3	24.1	2005	27.1	25.3
1978	24.2	21.8	1992	26.5	24.4	2006	27.5	25.5
1979	24.4	22.1	1993	26.5	24.5	2007	27.5	25.6
1980	24.7	22.0	1994	26.7	24.5	2008	27.6	25.9
1981	24.8	22.3	1995	26.9	24.5	2009	28.1	25.9
1982	25.2	22.5	1996	27.1	24.8	2010	28.2	26.1
1983	25.4	22.8	1997	26.8	25.0			

SOURCES: U.S. Census Bureau, *Current Population Reports*, series P20-514, "Marital Status and Living Arrangements: March 1998 (Update)," and earlier reports; U.S. Department of Labor, *Current Population Survey, March and Annual Social and Economic Supplements*, 2008 and earlier.

TABLE A3-4:

Marital Status of Women, Percentage Distribution, 1971–2010

Year	Divorced	Widowed	Married	Never Married	Year	Divorced	Widowed	Married	Never Married
1971	4.0%	13.8%	68.1%	14.1%	1991	9.6%	11.8%	59.3%	19.3%
1972	4.3%	13.4%	68.5%	13.8%	1992	9.9%	11.7%	59.1%	19.2%
1973	4.5%	13.5%	68.1%	13.9%	1993	10.1%	11.5%	59.2%	19.1%
1974	4.9%	13.3%	67.6%	14.3%	1994	10.2%	11.2%	58.8%	19.7%
1975	5.3%	13.4%	66.7%	14.6%	1995	10.3%	11.1%	59.2%	19.4%
1976	5.7%	13.1%	66.2%	15.0%	1996	10.5%	11.0%	58.6%	19.9%
1977	6.2%	12.9%	65.3%	15.6%	1997	11.0%	10.9%	57.9%	20.2%
1978	6.7%	12.7%	64.2%	16.4%	1998	10.8%	10.8%	57.9%	20.5%
1979	6.6%	13.0%	63.5%	16.9%	1999	10.7%	10.5%	57.7%	21.0%
1980	7.1%	12.8%	63.0%	17.1%	2000	10.8%	10.5%	57.6%	21.1%
1981	7.6%	12.7%	62.4%	17.4%	2001	11.1%	10.7%	57.4%	20.7%
1982	8.0%	12.5%	61.9%	17.6%	2002	11.3%	10.5%	57.1%	21.2%
1983	7.9%	12.4%	61.4%	18.3%	2003	11.5%	10.3%	57.1%	21.2%
1984	8.3%	12.5%	60.8%	18.4%	2004	11.5%	10.0%	57.1%	21.3%
1985	8.7%	12.6%	60.4%	18.2%	2005	11.5%	9.9%	56.9%	21.6%
1986	8.9%	12.4%	60.5%	18.3%	2006	11.6%	9.9%	56.5%	22.0%
1987	8.7%	12.1%	60.5%	18.6%	2007	11.5%	9.8%	56.7%	22.0%
1988	8.8%	12.1%	60.4%	18.7%	2008	11.1%	9.3%	50.3%	26.8%
1989	9.1%	12.2%	59.8%	18.9%	2009	10.8%	9.3%	50.6%	26.8%
1990	9.3%	12.1%	59.7%	18.9%	2010	11.1%	9.1%	49.9%	27.4%

NOTE: Women ages 18 and older.

SOURCES: U.S. Census Bureau, *Statistical Abstract*: 1971, no. 38; 1972, no. 46; 1980, no. 51; 1983, no. 44; 1989, no. 50; 1990, no. 50; 1991, no. 50; 1992, no. 49; 1993, no. 49; 1994, no. 59; 1995, no. 58; 1997, no. 58; 1998, no. 61; *Historical Statistics*, series A, pp. 160-71; U.S. Bureau of the Census, unpublished data; U.S. Census Bureau, 1970 Census of Population, vol. I, part 1, and Current Population Reports, P20-533, and earlier reports; and Families and Living Arrangements, 2008, 2009. http://www.census.gov/population/www/socdemo/hh-fam.html

TABLE A3-5

Share of All Births to Unmarried Women, by Race and Hispanic Origin, Selected Years 1960–2009

Year	Total	White	African American	Hispanic	Year	Total	White	African American	Hispanic
1960	5.3				1999	33.0	22.1	69.1	42.2
1965	7.7				2000	33.2	22.1	68.7	42.7
1970	10.7				2001	33.5	22.5	68.6	42.5
1975	14.3				2002	34.0	23.0	68.4	43.5
1980	18.4	9.6	57.3	23.6	2003	34.6	23.6	68.5	45.0
1985	22.0	12.4	62.1	29.5	2004	35.8	24.5	69.3	46.4
1990	28.0	16.9	66.7	36.7	2005	36.9	25.3	69.9	48.0
1995	32.2	21.2	70.0	40.8	2006	38.5	26.6	70.7	49.9
1996	32.4	21.5	70.0	40.7	2007	39.7	27.8	71.6	51.3
1997	32.4	21.5	69.4	40.9	2008	40.6	28.7	72.3	52.6
1998	32.8	21.9	69.3	41.6	2009	41.0	29.0	72.8	53.2

SOURCE: Child Trends Data Bank, 2009, http://www.childtrendsdatabank.org/sites/default/files/75_tab01.pdf.

TABLE A3-6:

Births per 1,000 Women Ages 15–44, 1970–2009

Year	Rate	Year	Rate	Year	Rate	Year	Rate
1970	87.9	1980	68.4	1990	70.9	2000	67.6
1971	81.8	1981	67.4	1991	69.6	2001	66.9
1972	73.4	1982	68.4	1992	68.9	2002	64.8
1973	69.2	1983	65.8	1993	67.6	2003	66.1
1974	68.4	1984	65.4	1994	66.7	2004	66.3
1975	66.7	1985	66.2	1995	65.6	2005	66.7
1976	65.8	1986	65.4	1996	65.3	2006	68.5
1977	67.8	1987	65.7	1997	65.0	2007	69.5
1978	66.6	1988	67.2	1998	65.6	2008	68.6
1979	68.5	1989	69.2	1999	65.8	2009	66.7

SOURCES: U.S. Census Bureau, *Historical Statistics*, vol. 1, series B28-35, p. 52; *Vital Statistics*: 1972, pp. 1-30; *Statistical Abstract*: 1980, no. 95; 1987, no. 86; 1990, no. 90; 1992, no. 89; 1994, no. 100; 1995, no. 94. *Monthly Vital Statistics Report*: 1997, vol. 45, no. 11(s), table 15; 1998, vol. 46, no. 11(s), table 17; *National Vital Statistics Report*: 1999, vol. 47, no. 25; 2000, vol. 48, no. 14; 2001, vol. 49, no. 5; 2002, vol. 51, no. 2; 2003, vol. 51, no. 11; 2005, vol. 54, no. 2; 2005, vol. 54, no. 8; 2007, vol. 56, no. 6; 2009, vol. 57, no. 7; 2009, vol. 57, no. 12; U.S. Centers for Disease Control, National Center for Health Statistics.

TABLE A3-7:

Percentage Distribution of Families with Children under 18 by Family Head, 1970–2010

Year	Married Couples	Mother Only	Father Only	Year	Married Couples	Mother Only	Father Only
1970	88.6%	10.2%	1.2%	1990	76.0%	20.4%	3.6%
1971	87.2%	11.7%	1.1%	1991	75.3%	21.1%	3.6%
1972	86.5%	12.2%	1.2%	1992	74.6%	21.5%	3.9%
1973	85.9%	12.8%	1.3%	1993	74.3%	21.7%	4.0%
1974	85.0%	13.7%	1.3%	1994	73.7%	22.5%	3.9%
1975	83.7%	14.7%	1.6%	1995	73.6%	22.2%	4.2%
1976	83.2%	15.3%	1.5%	1996	72.9%	22.4%	4.8%
1977	82.5%	15.9%	1.6%	1997	72.4%	22.7%	4.9%
1978	81.1%	17.1%	1.8%	1998	72.7%	22.1%	5.2%
1979	80.7%	17.4%	1.9%	1999	72.4%	22.7%	4.9%
1980	80.5%	17.5%	2.0%	2000	73.0%	21.9%	5.2%
1981	79.8%	18.0%	2.1%	2001	73.5%	21.3%	5.2%
1982	78.9%	18.9%	2.2%	2002	72.2%	22.4%	5.3%
1983	79.1%	18.6%	2.4%	2003	72.0%	22.6%	5.3%
1984	78.4%	19.0%	2.6%	2004	71.8%	22.9%	5.4%
1985	77.8%	19.3%	2.9%	2005	71.6%	22.8%	5.6%
1986	77.8%	19.3%	3.0%	2006	71.2%	23.0%	5.7%
1987	77.3%	19.7%	3.0%	2007	71.2%	23.4%	5.5%
1988	77.1%	19.7%	3.3%	2008	70.5%	23.5%	6.1%
1989	76.5%	20.2%	3.3%	2009	69.8%	22.8%	3.4%
				2010	69.3%	23.1%	3.4%

NOTE: Data for 1970 and 1980 include revisions from the Census Bureau.

SOURCE: U.S. Bureau of the Census, *Current Population Reports*, series P20-515, "Household and Family Characteristics: March 1998 (Update)," and earlier reports; U.S. Census Bureau, Current Population Survey, March and Annual Social and Economic Supplements, 2008 and earlier; U.S. Census Bureau, *American's Families and Living Arrangements* (2009).

TABLE A3-8:

Life Expectancy at Birth by Sex, 1970–2010 (age in years)

Year	Male	Female	Year	Male	Female	Year	Male	Female
1970	67.1	74.7	1983	71.0	78.1	1996	73.1	79.1
1971	67.4	75.0	1984	71.1	78.2	1997	73.6	79.4
1972	67.4	75.1	1985	71.1	78.2	1998	73.8	79.5
1973	67.6	75.3	1986	71.2	78.2	1999	73.9	79.4
1974	68.2	75.9	1987	71.4	78.3	2000	74.1	79.3
1975	68.8	76.6	1988	71.4	78.3	2001	74.2	79.4
1976	69.1	76.8	1989	71.7	78.5	2002	74.3	79.5
1977	69.5	77.2	1990	71.8	78.8	2003	74.5	79.6
1978	69.6	77.3	1991	72.0	78.9	2004	74.9	79.9
1979	70.0	77.8	1992	72.3	79.1	2005	74.9	79.9
1980	70.0	77.4	1993	72.2	78.8	2006	75.1	80.2
1981	70.4	77.8	1994	72.4	79.0	2007	75.3	80.4
1982	70.8	78.1	1995	72.5	78.9	2010	75.7	80.8

SOURCES: U.S. Census Bureau, *Historical Statistics*, vol. 1, series B, pp. 107-15; U.S. Centers for Disease Control, National Center for Health Statistics, *Health, United States*, 2008, table 26, p. 203; *National Vital Statistics Report*: 2009, vol. 57, no. 14; 2009, vol. 58, no. 1; *Statistical Abstract*, 1998, no. 128; *Vital Statistics*, 1985, no. 102; Famighetti (1997), 973.

TABLE A4-1:

Number of Women-Owned Businesses, 1997, 2002, and 2008

Year	Millions
1997	5.4
2002	6.5
2008	7.2

NOTE: Women-owned businesses are defined as firms in which women own at least 51 percent of interest or stocks in business.

SOURCES: U.S. Census Bureau, *1997 Survey of Women Business Enterprise; 2002 Survey of Business Owners*, Women-Owned Firms; Center for Women's Business Research, Biennial Update 2008: Businesses Owned by Women in the United States.

TABLE A4-2:

Industry Distribution of Women-Owned Firms, 2008

Industry	Percent
Health care and social services	17%
Professional, scientific, and technical services	15%
Retail trade	14%
Arts, entertainment, and recreational services	4%
Real Estate, rental, and leasing	7%
Educational services	3%
Administrative, support, waste management, and remediation services	9%
Other services	16%
Other industries	15%
TOTAL:	**100%**

SOURCE: Center for Women's Business Research, Biennial Update 2008: Businesses Owned by Women in the United States.

TABLE A5-1:

Women's Median Usual Weekly Earnings as a Percentage of Men's by Race and Ethnicity, 1979–2010

Year	White	African American	Asian	Hispanic	Year	White	African American	Asian	Hispanic
1979	61.7	74.4		71.7	1995	73.3	86.4		87.1
1980	63.4	75.8		73.5	1996	73.8	87.9		88.8
1981	63.1	76.9		75.7	1997	74.6	86.8		85.7
1982	64.5	78.1		75.5	1998	76.1	85.5		86.4
1983	65.6	78.9		78.5	1999	75.7	83.8		85.7
1984	66.8	79.5		77.7	2000	75.8	84.1	79.9	87.8
1985	67.2	82.6		77.7	2001	75.8	85.8	76.9	88.2
1986	67.9	82.8		80.6	2002	77.9	90.3	74.9	88.0
1987	68.2	84.4		82.0	2003	79.3	88.5	77.5	88.4
1988	68.4	82.8		84.4	2004	79.8	88.8	76.4	87.3
1989	69.3	86.5		85.4	2005	80.2	89.3	80.6	87.7
1990	71.5	85.3		87.4	2006	80.0	87.8	79.3	87.1
1991	73.7	86.1		90.4	2007	79.4	88.8	78.1	91.0
1992	75.3	88.2		89.1	2008	79.3	89.4	78.0	89.6
1993	76.5	88.8		90.5	2009	79.2	93.7	81.8	89.5
1994	74.6	86.5		88.9	2010	80.5	93.5	82.6	90.7

SOURCE: U.S. Department of Labor, Bureau of Labor Statistics, *Women in the Labor Force: A Databook* (2010), table 16; *Employment and Earnings* (January 2010), annual averages, table 37.

TABLE A5-2:

Women's Share of College Degrees Awarded to African Americans, 1977–2009

Year	Associate	Bachelor's	Master's	First Professional	Doctoral
1977	53.8%	57.1%	63.0%	30.6%	38.9%
1980	59.6%	59.6%	64.1%	39.5%	45.1%
1985	60.4%	59.9%	62.7%	46.4%	51.4%
1987	60.6%	60.2%	62.9%	46.3%	54.1%
1989	62.8%	61.5%	63.3%	48.6%	53.9%
1990	63.6%	61.9%	64.3%	51.0%	53.8%
1991	63.6%	62.6%	64.4%	53.2%	52.2%
1992	63.9%	62.7%	66.5%	54.7%	52.9%
1993	63.4%	62.9%	65.5%	56.4%	54.3%
1994	62.8%	63.3%	66.2%	57.2%	54.7%
1995	64.5%	63.6%	66.5%	56.2%	56.2%
1996	65.5%	64.0%	67.3%	57.9%	55.5%
1997	65.6%	64.4%	68.5%	58.5%	57.4%
1998	66.2%	64.9%	68.0%	58.0%	60.1%
1999	66.2%	65.9%	69.1%	58.8%	59.1%
2000	65.2%	65.7%	68.7%	58.4%	61.0%
2001	65.3%	65.8%	69.8%	61.0%	61.3%
2002	66.1%	66.4%	70.8%	61.7%	61.5%
2003	66.2%	66.6%	71.0%	62.0%	63.7%
2004	68.0%	66.6%	71.1%	62.1%	65.0%
2005	68.6%	66.3%	71.1%	64.2%	65.7%
2006	69.2%	66.2%	71.2%	63.2%	65.4%
2007	69.1%	66.1%	71.4%	63.4%	65.6%
2008	68.6%	65.7%	71.8%	62.7%	66.4%
2009	68.5%	65.8%	71.8%	61.9%	66.5%

SOURCE: U.S. Department of Education, National Center for Education Statistics, *Digest of Education Statistics 2009* (2010).

TABLE A5-3:

African American Labor Force Participation Rate by Sex, 1972–2011

Year	Adult Men	Adult Women	Year	Adult Men	Adult Women	Year	Adult Men	Adult Women
1972	73.6%	48.7%	1985	70.8%	56.5%	1998	69.0%	62.8%
1973	73.4%	49.3%	1986	71.2%	56.9%	1999	68.7%	63.5%
1974	72.9%	49.0%	1987	71.1%	58.0%	2000	69.2%	63.1%
1975	70.9%	48.8%	1988	71.0%	58.0%	2001	68.4%	62.8%
1976	70.0%	49.8%	1989	71.0%	58.7%	2002	68.4%	61.8%
1977	70.6%	50.8%	1990	71.0%	58.3%	2003	67.3%	61.9%
1978	71.5%	53.1%	1991	70.4%	57.5%	2004	66.7%	61.5%
1979	71.3%	53.1%	1992	70.7%	58.5%	2005	67.3%	61.6%
1980	70.3%	53.1%	1993	69.6%	57.9%	2006	67.0%	61.7%
1981	70.0%	53.5%	1994	69.1%	58.7%	2007	66.8%	61.1%
1982	70.1%	53.7%	1995	69.0%	59.5%	2008	66.7%	61.3%
1983	70.6%	54.2%	1996	68.7%	60.4%	2009	65.0%	60.3%
1984	70.8%	55.2%	1997	68.3%	61.7%	2010	65.0%	59.9%
						2011	64.2%	59.1%

SOURCE: U.S. Department of Labor, Bureau of Labor Statistics, Current Population Survey.

TABLE A5-4:

African American Unemployment Rates by Sex, 1972–2011

Year	Adult Men	Adult Women	Year	Adult Men	Adult Women	Year	Adult Men	Adult Women
1972	9.3%	11.8%	1985	15.3%	14.9%	1998	8.9%	9.0%
1973	8.0%	11.1%	1986	14.8%	14.2%	1999	8.2%	7.8%
1974	9.8%	11.3%	1987	12.7%	13.2%	2000	8.0%	7.1%
1975	14.8%	14.8%	1988	11.7%	11.7%	2001	9.3%	8.1%
1976	13.7%	14.3%	1989	11.5%	11.4%	2002	10.7%	9.8%
1977	13.3%	14.9%	1990	11.9%	10.9%	2003	11.6%	10.2%
1978	11.8%	13.8%	1991	13.0%	12.0%	2004	11.1%	9.8%
1979	11.4%	13.3%	1992	15.2%	13.2%	2005	10.5%	9.5%
1980	14.5%	14.0%	1993	13.8%	12.1%	2006	9.5%	8.4%
1981	15.7%	15.6%	1994	12.0%	11.0%	2007	9.1%	7.5%
1982	20.1%	17.6%	1995	10.6%	10.2%	2008	11.4%	8.9%
1983	20.3%	18.6%	1996	11.1%	10.0%	2009	17.5%	12.4%
1984	16.4%	15.4%	1997	10.2%	9.9%	2010	18.4%	13.8%
						2011	17.8%	14.1%

SOURCE: U.S. Department of Labor, Bureau of Labor Statistics, Current Population Survey.

TABLE A5-5:

Women's Median Income by Race and Ethnicity (2009 dollars), 1948–2009

Year	White	African American	Asian	Hispanic	Year	White	African American	Asian	Hispanic
1948	8,812	3,827			1981	12,489	11,095		11,450
1949	8,426	3,898			1982	12,734	11,232		10,970
1950	8,244	3,687			1983	13,142	11,345		11,057
1951	8,801	3,734			1984	13,664	12,120		11,463
1952	9,478	3,660			1985	13,986	11,933		11,444
1953	9,091	5,323			1986	14,490	12,260		11,834
1954	8,983	4,871			1987	15,365	12,551		11,975
1955	8,764	4,571			1988	15,860	12,804	16,105	12,178
1956	8,719	5,011			1989	16,388	13,153	18,721	12,772
1957	8,763	5,072			1990	16,413	13,249	17,637	11,983
1958	8,307	4,871			1991	16,466	13,540	16,934	12,307
1959	8,452	5,205			1992	16,421	13,311	17,781	12,444
1960	8,569	5,305			1993	16,468	13,898	18,074	11,840
1961	8,509	5,704			1994	16,644	15,090	17,692	12,327
1962	8,779	5,896			1995	17,212	15,318	17,975	12,477
1963	8,813	5,902			1996	17,644	16,025	19,921	12,910
1964	9,178	6,439			1997	18,378	17,386	19,071	13,671
1965	9,605	6,991			1998	19,209	17,264	20,012	14,274
1966	9,931	7,557			1999	19,762	19,021	21,623	14,644
1967	10,416	8,198			2000	20,027	19,781	21,618	15,256
1968	11,233	8,910			2001	20,175	19,726	22,444	15,245
1969	11,286	9,517			2002	20,076	19,946	21,565	15,934
1970	11,170	10,170			2003	20,318	19,337	20,618	15,910
1971	11,561	10,130			2004	20,098	19,712	23,304	16,411
1972	11,995	11,206			2005	20,512	19,371	23,777	16,520
1973	12,181	10,995			2006	21,364	20,322	23,618	16,764
1974	12,227	11,039			2007	21,796	20,433	25,195	17,326
1975	12,397	11,262			2008	20,870	20,120	23,021	16,355
1976	12,360	11,647			2009	21,118	19,470	24,343	16,210
1977	12,900	11,139							
1978	12,422	11,185							
1979	12,096	11,008							
1980	12,260	11,351							

NOTE: Women ages 15 and older.
SOURCE: U.S. Census Bureau, Current Population Survey, Annual Social and Economic Supplements.

TABLE A5-6:

Women's Share of College Degrees Awarded to Hispanic Americans, 1977–2009

Year	Associate	Bachelor's	Master's	First Professional	Doctoral
1977	45.3%	45.0%	46.2%	17.0%	26.6%
1980	53.2%	50.5%	52.3%	26.6%	39.3%
1985	55.9%	52.1%	55.4%	34.2%	36.3%
1987	54.7%	52.3%	52.7%	36.5%	41.3%
1989	54.8%	53.4%	54.3%	39.4%	44.4%
1990	56.4%	54.5%	55.0%	40.2%	46.3%
1991	58.0%	55.6%	55.7%	40.4%	47.3%
1992	57.2%	55.8%	55.7%	40.9%	43.6%
1993	57.0%	56.2%	55.6%	40.9%	47.0%
1994	58.9%	56.6%	57.1%	43.1%	48.6%
1995	56.4%	56.4%	57.5%	43.2%	50.4%
1996	58.9%	57.1%	59.5%	44.0%	48.4%
1997	58.7%	57.9%	59.5%	45.1%	47.8%
1998	58.3%	58.1%	59.9%	44.5%	48.9%
1999	60.2%	59.1%	60.6%	46.6%	52.0%
2000	59.4%	59.6%	60.3%	45.8%	53.2%
2001	59.2%	59.7%	61.6%	48.1%	54.7%
2002	60.1%	60.3%	62.3%	48.4%	54.7%
2003	60.3%	60.6%	63.0%	49.9%	52.6%
2004	61.5%	60.6%	63.6%	51.3%	53.9%
2005	62.2%	60.9%	63.8%	50.2%	58.1%
2006	62.8%	61.1%	64.1%	52.2%	56.1%
2007	62.9%	61.1%	64.5%	51.8%	56.1%
2008	63.0%	61.1%	64.5%	52.5%	57.1%
2009	62.5%	60.9%	63.9%	52.8%	57.0%

SOURCE: U.S. Department of Education, National Center for Education Statistics, *Digest of Education Statistics 2009* (2010).

TABLE A5-7:

Hispanic American Labor Force Participation Rates by Sex, 1973–2011

Year	Men	Women	Year	Men	Women	Year	Men	Women
1973	81.5%	41.0%	1986	81.0%	50.1%	1999	79.8%	55.9%
1974	81.7%	42.4%	1987	81.0%	52.0%	2000	81.5%	57.5%
1975	80.7%	43.2%	1988	81.9%	53.2%	2001	81.0%	57.6%
1976	79.6%	44.3%	1989	82.0%	53.5%	2002	80.2%	57.6%
1977	80.9%	44.3%	1990	81.4%	53.1%	2003	80.1%	55.9%
1978	81.1%	46.6%	1991	80.3%	52.4%	2004	80.4%	56.1%
1979	81.3%	47.4%	1992	80.7%	52.8%	2005	80.1%	55.3%
1980	81.4%	47.4%	1993	80.2%	51.1%	2006	80.7%	56.1%
1981	80.6%	48.3%	1994	79.2%	52.9%	2007	80.5%	56.5%
1982	79.7%	48.1%	1995	79.1%	52.6%	2008	80.2%	56.2%
1983	80.3%	47.7%	1996	79.6%	53.4%	2009	78.8%	56.5%
1984	80.6%	49.7%	1997	80.1%	55.1%	2010	77.8%	56.5%
1985	80.4%	49.3%	1998	79.8%	55.6%	2011	76.2%	55.5%

SOURCE: U.S. Department of Labor, Bureau of Labor Statistics, Current Population Survey.

TABLE A5-8:

Hispanic American Unemployment Rates by Sex, 1973–2011

Year	Men	Women	Year	Men	Women	Year	Men	Women
1973	6.7%	9.0%	1986	10.5%	10.8%	1999	5.6%	7.6%
1974	7.3%	9.4%	1987	8.7%	8.9%	2000	5.0%	6.8%
1975	11.4%	13.5%	1988	8.1%	8.3%	2001	5.9%	7.5%
1976	10.8%	12.7%	1989	7.6%	8.8%	2002	7.2%	8.0%
1977	9.0%	11.9%	1990	8.0%	8.4%	2003	7.2%	8.4%
1978	7.7%	11.3%	1991	10.3%	9.6%	2004	6.5%	7.6%
1979	7.0%	10.3%	1992	11.7%	11.4%	2005	5.4%	6.9%
1980	9.7%	10.7%	1993	10.6%	11.0%	2006	4.8%	5.9%
1981	10.2%	10.8%	1994	9.4%	10.7%	2007	5.3%	6.1%
1982	13.6%	14.1%	1995	8.8%	10.0%	2008	7.6%	7.7%
1983	13.6%	13.8%	1996	7.9%	10.2%	2009	12.5%	11.5%
1984	10.5%	11.1%	1997	7.0%	8.9%	2010	12.7%	12.3%
1985	10.2%	11.0%	1998	6.4%	8.2%	2011	12.9%	11.9%

SOURCE: U.S. Department of Labor, Bureau of Labor Statistics, Current Population Survey.

TABLE A5-9:

Share of College Degrees Awarded to Asian American Women, 1977–2009

Year	Associate	Bachelor's	Master's	First Professional	Doctoral
1977	48.5%	44.6%	39.0%	24.0%	17.9%
1980	47.3%	46.2%	39.9%	31.9%	25.3%
1985	44.6%	46.6%	37.8%	36.6%	27.5%
1987	47.6%	47.1%	38.8%	37.4%	27.7%
1989	49.1%	48.9%	41.5%	38.9%	28.6%
1990	52.8%	49.8%	43.5%	41.6%	29.4%
1991	53.0%	50.1%	43.6%	42.3%	32.4%
1992	53.5%	50.1%	44.2%	42.7%	31.9%
1993	52.7%	50.8%	45.6%	44.5%	34.1%
1994	55.1%	51.6%	46.2%	45.5%	32.2%
1995	55.3%	52.1%	47.0%	45.4%	34.7%
1996	55.8%	52.4%	48.4%	46.6%	35.9%
1997	56.5%	52.8%	51.6%	46.3%	38.3%
1998	56.5%	53.3%	51.4%	48.2%	40.5%
1999	57.7%	53.9%	52.5%	46.8%	41.8%
2000	56.8%	54.0%	52.4%	49.1%	44.0%
2001	56.6%	54.5%	53.3%	51.2%	43.8%
2002	57.2%	54.7%	53.8%	51.9%	46.4%
2003	56.9%	54.3%	54.1%	52.8%	48.7%
2004	58.0%	55.1%	53.6%	54.6%	50.9%
2005	59.0%	55.0%	54.2%	55.2%	51.8%
2006	59.6%	55.3%	53.6%	56.4%	52.3%
2007	58.4%	54.8%	54.5%	55.9%	51.9%
2008	59.0%	54.6%	53.9%	56.7%	55.0%
2009	58.0%	54.9%	53.7%	56.0%	54.3%

SOURCE: U.S. Department of Education, National Center for Education Statistics, *Digest of Education Statistics 2009* (2010).

TABLE A5-10:

Asian American Labor Force Participation Rates by Sex, 2000–2011

Year	Men	Women	Year	Men	Women	Year	Men	Women
2000	76.1%	59.2%	2004	75.0%	57.6%	2008	75.3%	59.4%
2001	76.2%	59.0%	2005	74.8%	58.2%	2009	74.6%	58.2%
2002	75.9%	59.1%	2006	75.0%	58.3%	2010	73.2%	57.0%
2003	75.6%	58.3%	2007	75.1%	58.6%	2011	73.73%	57.1%

SOURCE: U.S. Department of Labor, Bureau of Labor Statistics, Current Population Survey.

TABLE A5-11:

Asian American Unemployment Rates by Sex, 2000–2011

Year	Men	Women	Year	Men	Women	Year	Men	Women
2000	3.6%	3.6%	2004	4.5%	4.3%	2008	4.1%	3.7%
2001	4.5%	4.4%	2005	4.0%	3.9%	2009	7.9%	6.6%
2002	6.1%	5.7%	2006	3.0%	3.1%	2010	7.8%	7.1%
2003	6.2%	5.7%	2007	3.1%	3.4%	2011	6.6%	7.3%

SOURCE: U.S. Department of Labor, Bureau of Labor Statistics, Current Population Survey.

TABLE A5-12:

Mothers' Labor Force Participation Rates, 1996–2010

Year	White	African American	Asian	Hispanic	Year	White	African American	Asian	Hispanic
1996	70.7%	73.3%		56.7%	2003	70.3%	77.5%	67.0%	61.2%
1997	71.7%	75.0%		59.6%	2004	69.8%	76.5%	64.9%	60.4%
1998	71.3%	76.7%		60.2%	2005	69.8%	76.3%	65.6%	59.6%
1999	71.5%	78.5%		60.3%	2006	70.2%	76.9%	66.3%	60.9%
2000	71.6%	78.2%		62.0%	2007	70.3%	76.6%	67.1%	61.4%
2001	71.5%	77.9%		62.0%	2008	70.8%	76.7%	68.8%	61.4%
2002	71.1%	77.7%	66.6%	62.7%	2009	70.9%	76.3%	68.0%	61.5%
					2010	70.5%	74.9%	66.2%	62.1%

SOURCE: U.S. Department of Labor, Bureau of Labor Statistics, *Labor Force Characteristics by Race and Ethnicity, 2009* (August 2010), tables 2 and 9.

TABLE A5-13:

Ratio of Women to Men in Management, Professional, and Related Occupations by Race, 1994–2010

Year	White	African American	Asian	Hispanic	Year	White	African American	Asian	Hispanic
1994	0.900	1.406			2003	0.985	1.661	0.793	0.991
1995	0.895	1.333			2004	0.976	1.631	0.802	1.048
1996	0.921	1.480			2005	0.989	1.650	0.796	1.059
1997	0.933	1.485			2006	0.992	1.594	0.804	1.048
1998	0.930	1.526			2007	0.993	1.595	0.816	1.059
1999	0.946	1.555			2008	1.007	1.573	0.802	1.049
2000	0.959	1.522			2009	1.024	1.704	0.826	1.064
2001	0.973	1.580			2010	1.025	1.706	0.839	1.082
2002	0.994	1.608	0.744	1.077					

SOURCE: U.S. Census Bureau, Current Population Survey, CPS Household Data, Table 10 (1994–2010).

TABLE A5-14:

Women Employed in Management, Business, and Financial Operations Occupations as a Percentage of the Total Number of Employed Women by Race, 1994–2010

Year	White	African American	Asian	Hispanic	Year	White	African American	Asian	Hispanic
1994	29.8%	21.3%			2003	38.4%	30.9%	42.9%	21.1%
1995	30.6%	22.1%			2004	38.6%	30.6%	43.8%	22.4%
1996	31.5%	22.8%			2005	38.8%	30.4%	44.5%	22.4%
1997	32.0%	22.4%			2006	38.9%	31.1%	45.7%	22.1%
1998	32.6%	23.2%			2007	39.5%	31.2%	46.8%	23.1%
1999	33.4%	24.5%			2008	40.6%	31.3%	46.0%	23.5%
2000	33.4%	24.8%			2009	41.4%	33.7%	47.7%	24.6%
2001	34.4%	26.0%			2010	41.5%	33.8%	46.1%	24.1%
2002	38.0%	30.5%	40.1%	21.7%					

SOURCE: U.S. Census Bureau, Current Population Survey, CPS Household Data, Table 10 (1994–2010).

TABLE A6-1:

Labor Force Participation Rates of Women, 1970, 1990, and 2010

	1970	1990	2010
United States	43.3%	57.5%	58.6%
Canada	38.3%	58.5%	62.4%
Australia	40.4%	53.2%	59.8%
Japan	48.7%	49.1%	48.1%
France	39.8%	46.4%	51.7%
Germany	38.4%	43.6%	51.6%
Italy	26.4%	32.7%	38.3%
Netherlands*	28.5%	44.2%	58.8%
Sweden	50.0%	63.0%	60.4%
United Kingdom**	44.6%	54.0%	56.8%

*1973 Rate for Netherlands

**1971 Rate for United Kingdom

SOURCE: U.S. Department of Labor, Bureau of Labor Statistics, Division of International Labor Comparisons, *International Comparison of Annual Labor Force Statistics*, Table 3-5, http://www.bls.gov/fls/flscomparelf/lfcompendium.pdf.

TABLE A6-2:

Unemployment Rates for Women, 1970–2010

	U.S.	Canada	Australia	Japan	France	Germany	Italy	Netherlands	Sweden	U.K.
1970	4.4	5.6	1.1	1.2	1.5	0.5		2.5	1.4	
1971	5.3	6.0	1.3	1.2	1.7	0.5	2.5	2.4	3.6	
1972	5.0	5.8	1.9	1.5	1.8	0.7	2.9	2.5	3.9	
1973	4.2	4.9	1.6	1.3	1.6	0.6	2.7	2.6	2.2	3.0
1974	4.9	4.8	1.9	1.4	1.8	1.5	2.3	2.8	1.7	3.0
1975	7.9	6.2	3.8	1.8	2.7	3.3	2.5	3.9	1.4	4.1
1976	7.1	6.3	3.9	2.2	2.9	3.0	2.7	4.1	1.3	5.2
1977	6.3	7.3	4.6	2.0	3.3	2.9	2.8	3.8	1.5	5.3
1978	5.3	7.5	5.4	2.2	3.5	2.7	2.8	3.6	2.1	5.1
1979	5.1	6.7	5.2	1.9	3.9	2.3	3.0	3.6	1.9	4.9
1980	6.9	6.9	5.1	1.7	4.0	2.3	2.9	4.2	1.7	6.7
1981	7.4	7.0	4.8	2.0	5.0	3.3	3.3	6.9	2.4	10.3
1982	9.9	11.1	6.4	2.1	5.6	5.0	3.8	8.6	3.0	11.6
1983	9.9	12.2	9.7	2.5	6.0	6.2	4.1	10.4	3.4	12.3
1984	7.4	11.1	8.7	2.5	7.4	6.2	4.2	10.4	3.0	12.0
1985	7.0	10.4	7.9	2.2	8.0	6.2	4.2	8.4	2.8	11.8
1986	6.9	9.4	7.6	2.4	8.0	5.5	5.2	7.9	2.6	11.8
1987	6.2	8.3	7.6	2.2	7.9	5.4	5.5	7.3	2.3	10.9
1988	5.5	7.2	6.6	2.0	7.4	5.3	5.5	7.3	1.9	8.9
1989	5.2	7.0	5.6	1.8	6.6	4.6	5.4	6.4	1.6	7.4
1990	5.7	7.9	6.6	1.7	6.5	4.2	4.8	5.6	1.9	7.4
1991	7.2	10.5	9.7	1.7	6.7	4.6	4.9	5.4	3.5	9.9
1992	7.9	11.6	11.2	1.8	7.7	5.5	5.3	5.4	6.8	11.8
1993	7.2	11.5	11.3	2.1	9.1	6.7	7.4	5.3	11.0	12.4
1994	6.2	10.2	9.8	2.3	9.8	7.3	8.4	6.1	11.0	11.3
1995	5.6	9.1	8.6	2.6	9.0	7.3	8.7	5.9	9.9	10.1
1996	5.4	9.2	8.5	2.8	9.7	8.4	8.8	5.3	10.4	9.5
1997	4.9	8.7	8.5	2.8	9.9	9.4	8.8	4.5	10.4	7.9
1998	4.4	8.1	8.0	3.5	9.3	8.9	8.9	3.5	8.7	7.0
1999	4.1	7.3	7.1	4.0	8.9	8.1	8.6	2.8	7.4	6.6
2000	3.9	6.3	6.5	4.1	7.4	7.6	7.9	2.3	6.2	6.0
2001	4.8	6.9	7.0	4.4	6.6	7.8	7.2	1.8	5.3	5.7
2002	5.9	7.5	6.5	4.7	7.2	8.8	6.8	2.5	5.6	5.8
2003	6.3	7.3	5.9	4.3	7.8	9.7	6.6	3.5	6.3	5.6
2004	5.6	6.8	5.3	3.9	8.2	10.6	6.5	4.4	6.9	5.2
2005	5.0	6.3	4.9	3.5	8.2	11.5	6.3	4.5	7.8	5.3
2006	4.6	5.8	4.7	3.3	8.2	10.5	5.5	3.6	6.9	5.8
2007	4.7	5.6	4.0	3.2	7.6	8.6	5.0	2.8	5.8	5.7
2008	6.1	5.8	4.0	3.4	7.0	7.5	5.6	2.6	5.8	6.2
2009	8.1	6.1	5.4	5.2	9.4	7.3	9.3	3.8	7.9	6.5
2010	8.6	6.2	5.4	5.0	9.7	6.7	9.8	4.5	8.2	6.9

SOURCE: U.S. Department of Labor, Bureau of Labor Statistics, Division of International Labor Comparisons, *International Comparison of Annual Labor Force Statistics*, Table 1-4 .

TABLE A6-3:

Total Fertility Rates, 1960, 1980, and 2009

(Number of Children per Woman of Child-Bearing Age)

Country	1960	1980	2009
United States	3.65	1.84	2.01
United Kingdom	2.72	1.90	1.94
Spain	2.86	2.22	1.40
Mexico	7.25	4.97	2.08
Korea	6.00	2.82	1.15
Japan	2.00	1.75	1.37
Italy	2.41	1.68	1.41
Germany	2.37	1.56	1.36
France	2.74	1.95	1.99
Canada	3.90	1.68	1.66
Australia	3.45	1.89	1.90

SOURCE: Organisation for Economic Co-operation and Development, *OECD Family Database* (2010).

TABLE A6-4:

Mean Age of Women at the Birth of First Child, 1995

Country	Mean Age
Mexico	21.0
United States	24.5
Canada	26.4
Australia	26.9
France	28.1
Japan	27.5
Korea	26.5
Spain	28.4
Italy	28.0
Germany	27.5
United Kingdom	28.3

SOURCE: Organisation for Economic Co-operation and Development, *OECD Family Database* (2011).

TABLE A6-5:

Mean Age of Women at Birth of First Child, 2008

Country	Mean Age
Mexico	21.3
United States	25.0
Canada	27.6
Australia	28.0
France	28.6
Italy	29.9
Japan	29.1
Korea	29.1
Germany	30.0
Spain	29.7
United Kingdom	30.0

SOURCE: Organisation for Economic Co-operation and Development, *OECD Family Database* (2010).

TABLE A6-6:

Women's Labor Force Participation Rates, 2010

Country	Rate
United States	58.6%
Canada	62.4%
Australia	59.8%
Japan	48.1%
France	51.7%
Germany	58.8%
Italy	51.6%
Netherlands	38.3%
Sweden	60.4%
United Kingdom	56.8%

SOURCE: Bureau of Labor Statistics: International Comparisons of Annual Labor Force Statistics, Adjusted to U.S. Concepts, 10 Countries, 1970-2010.

TABLE A6-7:

Women's Share of Students in Higher Education, 2000, 2005, and 2015

Country	2000	2005	2015*
Australia	54%	54%	55%
Canada	56%	58%	60%
France	54%	55%	56%
Germany	48%	50%	54%
Italy	56%	57%	57%
Japan	45%	46%	47%
Korea	36%	37%	38%
Netherlands	50%	51%	53%
Sweden	58%	60%	62%
Spain	53%	54%	55%
United Kingdom	54%	57%	65%
United States	56%	57%	60%
Mexico	49%	50%	52%

*Projections

SOURCE: Organisation for Economic Co-operation and Development, *Higher Education to 2030*, Vol. 1, *Demography* (2008).

TABLE A6-8:

Women's Share of College Degrees, 2005 and 2015

Country	2005	2015*
Australia	56%	62%
Canada	59%	59%
France	56%	65%
Germany	53%	65%
Italy	59%	68%
Japan	49%	49%
Korea	49%	54%
Netherlands	56%	70%
Sweden	63%	74%
Spain	58%	64%
United Kingdom	58%	72%
United States	58%	61%
Mexico	55%	46%

*2015 Projections

SOURCE: Organisation for Economic Co-operation and Development, *Higher Education to 2030*, Vol. 1, *Demography* (2008).

TABLE A7-1:

Revenue and Expenses of Selected Women's Organizations, 2008/2009

Organization/Year	Revenue	Expenses
NOW Foundation (2009)	$243,001	$578,570
NOW (2009)	$3,264,803	$2,600,310
AAUW Educational Foundation (2008)	$13,313,002	$13,056,231
AAUW Action Fund (2008)	$286,842	$1,009,007
NWLC (2008)	$9,111,765	$8,175,221
Catalyst (2008)	$8,709,441	$8,176,396

SOURCES: National Organization for Women, Inc., *U.S. Internal Revenue Service 2009 Form 990* (2010); American Association of University Women, *U.S. Internal Revenue Service 2009 Form 990* (2010); National Women's Law Center, *U.S. Internal Revenue Service 2000 Form 990* (2010); and Catalyst, Inc., *U.S. Internal Revenue Service 2009 Form 990* (2010).

TABLE A7-2:

National Organization for Women Revenue, 2009

Source of Revenue	Amount of Revenue	Share of Total Revenue
Contributions, gifts, and grants	$3,317,509	97.2%
Program service revenue	$29,979	0.9%
List rental income	$33,772	1.0%
Other income	$28,762	0.8%
Royalties	$2,524	0.1%
TOTAL:	**$3,412,546**	**100.0%**

SOURCE: National Organization for Women, Inc., *U.S. Internal Revenue Service 2009 Form 990* (2010);

TABLE A7-3:

American Association of University Women Educational Foundation Revenue, 2009

Source of Revenue	Amount of Revenue	Share of Total Revenue
Contributions, gifts, grants	$8,347,226	62.7%
Program service revenue	$367,848	2.8%
Dividends and interest from securities	$2,424,436	18.2%
Royalties	$41,975	0.3%
Net rental income	$124,332	0.9%
Non-inventory sales	$1,796,899	13.5%
Other revenue	$210,286	1.6%
TOTAL:	**$13,313,002**	**100.0%**

SOURCE: American Association of University Women, *U.S. Internal Revenue Service 2009 Form 990* (2010).

TABLE A7-4:

American Association of University Women Action Fund Revenue, 2009

Source of Revenue	Amount of Revenue	Share of Total Revenue
Contributions, gifts, grants	$410	0.1%
Program service revenue	$198,502	67.2%
Dividends and interest from securities	$72,367	24.5%
Royalties	$24,158	8.2%
TOTAL:	**$295,437**	**100.0%**

SOURCE: American Association of University Women, *U.S. Internal Revenue Service 2009 Form 990* (2010).

TABLE A7-5:

National Women's Law Center Revenue, 2009

Source of Revenue	Amount of Revenue	Share of Total Revenue
Contributions, gifts, grants	$8,151,113	82.6%
Program service revenue	$1,187,466	12.0%
Dividends and interest from securities	$394,328	4.0%
Fundraising	$2,882	0.0%
Sublease income	$128,630	1.3%
Other revenue	$2,229	0.0%
TOTAL:	**$9,866,648**	**100.0%**

SOURCE: National Women's Law Center, *U.S. Internal Revenue Service 2009 Form 990* (2010).

TABLE A7-6:

Catalyst Revenue, 2009

Source of Revenue	Amount of Revenue	Share of Total Revenue
Contributions, gifts, grants	$7,602,550	86.2%
Program service revenue	$822,052	9.3%
Interest on savings/temp cash investments	$386,533	4.4%
Fundraising	$5,363	0.1%
TOTAL:	**$8,816,498**	**100.0%**

SOURCE: Catalyst, Inc., *U.S. Internal Revenue Service 2009 Form 990* (2010).

References

Albelda, Randy. 2009. *Equal Pay for Equal Work? New Evidence on the Persistence of the Gender Pay Gap*. Statement at the House of Representatives, Joint Economic Committee. April 28, 2009.

American Association of University Women. 2008. U.S. Internal Revenue Service 2007 Form 990.

———. AAUW Research. http://www.aauw.org/learn/research/ (accessed July 29, 2010).

———. AAUW's Organizational Structure. http://www.aauw.org/about/aauw.cfm (accessed July 29, 2010).

———. About AAUW. http://www.aauw.org/about/ (accessed August 3, 2010).

———. Current Research Reports. http://www.aauw.org/learn/research/current.cfm (accessed July 30, 2010).

———. Position on Science and Math Education. http://www.aauw.org/actissue_advocacy/actionpages/STEM.cfm (accessed August 3, 2010).

———. Principles and Priorities. http://www.aauw.org/act/issue_advocacy/principles_priorities.cfm (accessed July 30, 2010).

———. *Pay Equity and Workplace Opportunity: A Simple Matter of Fairness*. 2007.

American Association of University Women Educational Foundation, Inc. 2008. U.S. Internal Revenue Service 2007 Form 990.

Autor, David, and David Dorn. 2009. *Inequality and Specialization: The Growth of Low-Skill Service Jobs in the United States*. Working Paper No. 15150, National Bureau of Economic Research.

Babcock, Linda, and Sara Laschever. 2003. *Women Don't Ask*. Princeton: Princeton University Press.

Baron, Lisa. 2003. Ask and you shall receive: Gender differences in negotiators' beliefs about requests for a higher salary. *Human Relations* 56: 635–62.

Beller, Andrea H. 1982. Occupational Segregation by Sex: Determinants and Changes. *Journal of Human Resources* 17 (Summer): 371–92.

Beller, Andrea H., and Francine D. Blau. 1988. Trends in Earnings Differentials by Gender: 1971–1981. *Industrial and Labor Relations Review* 41 (4): 513–29.

Bertola, Giuseppe, Francine D. Blau, and Lawrence M. Kahn. 2007. Labor Market Institutions and Demographic Employment Patterns. *Journal of Population Economics* 20 (4): 833–67.

Bertrand, Marianne, Claudia Goldin, and Lawrence F. Katz. 2010. Dynamics of the Gender Gap for Young Professionals in the Financial and Corporate Sectors. *American Economic Journal: Applied Economics*, 2 (3): 228–55.

———. 2009. *Dynamics of the Gender Gap for Young Professionals in the Corporate and Financial Sectors*. Working Paper No. 14681, National Bureau for Economic Research.

Bertrand, Marianne, and Kevin Hallock. 2001. The Gender Gap in Top Corporate Jobs. *Industrial and Labor Relations Review* 55 (1): 3–21.

Black, Sandra E., and Alexandra Spitz-Oener. 2010. Explaining Women's Success: Technological Change and the Skill Content of Women's Work. *Review of Economics and Statistics* 92 (1): 187–94.

Black, Sandra E., and Elizabeth Brainerd. 2002. *Importing Equality? The Impact of Globalization on Gender Discrimination.* Working Paper No. 9110, National Bureau of Economic Research.

Blau, Francine D. 1993. Gender and Economic Outcomes: The Role of Wage Structure. *Labour: Review of Labour Economics and Industrial Relations* 7 (1): 73–92.

Blau, Francine D., and Jed DeVaro. 2007. New Evidence on Gender Differences in Promotion Rates: An Empirical Analysis of a Sample of New Hires. *Industrial Relations Review* 46 (3): 511–50.

Blau, Francine D., and Marianne A. Ferber. 1991. Career Plans and Expectations of Young Women and Men: The Earnings Gap and Labor Force Participation. *Journal of Human Resources* 26 (4): 581–607.

———. 1992. *The Economics of Men, Women, and Work.* 2nd ed. Englewood Cliffs, New Jersey: Prentice-Hall.

Blau, Francine D., and Adam J. Grossberg. 1991. Wage and Employment Uncertainty and the Labor Force Participation Decisions of Married Women. *Economic Inquiry* 29 (4): 678–95.

Blau, Francine D., and Wallace Hendriks. 1979. Occupational Segregation by Sex: Trends and Prospects. *Journal of Human Resources* 14 (2): 197–210.

Blau, Francine D., and Lawrence M. Kahn. 1994. Rising Wage Inequality and the U.S. Gender Gap. *American Economic Review* 84 (2): 23–8.

———. 1996. Wage Structure and Gender Earnings Differentials: an International Comparison. *Economica* 63 (250): S29–S62.

———. 1997. Swimming Upstream: Trends in the Gender Wage Differential in the 1980s. *Journal of Labor Economics* 15 (1): 1–42.

———. 1999. Analyzing the Gender Pay Gap. *Quarterly Review of Economics and Finance* 139 (special issue): 625–46.

———. 2002. Gender Differences in Pay. *Journal of Economic Perspectives* 14 (4): 75–99.

———. 2003. Understanding International Differences in the Gender Pay Gap. *Journal of Labor Economics* 21 (1): 106–44.

———. 2005. Do Cognitive Test Scores Explain Higher U.S. Wage Inequality? *Review of Economics and Statistics* 87 (1): 184–93.

———. 2006. The U.S. Gender Pay Gap in the 1990s: Slowing Convergence. *Industrial and Labor Relations Review* 60 (1): 45–66.

———. 2007a. The Gender Pay Gap: Have Women Gone as Far as They Can?—*Academy of Management Perspectives* 21 (1): 7–23.

———. 2007b. Changes in the Labor Supply Behavior of Married Women: 1980–2000. *Journal of Labor Economics* 25 (3): 393–438.

———. 2007c. The Gender Pay Gap.—*The Economists' Voice* 4 (4, article 5).

Blau, Francine D., Lawrence M. Kahn, and Jane Waldfogel. 2000. Understanding Young Women's Marriage Decisions: The Role of Labor and Marriage Market Conditions. *Industrial and Labor Relations Review* 53 (4): 624–47.

Blau, Francine D., Patricia Simpson, and Deborah Anderson. 1998. Continuing Progress? Trends in Occupational Segregation–Over the 1970s and 1980s. *Feminist Economics* 4(3): 29–71.

Brown, Charles, and Mary Corcoran. 1997. Sex Based Differences in School Content and the Male/Female Wage Gap. *Journal of Labor Economics*, 15 (3): 431–65.

California National Organization for Women, Inc. 2010. U.S. Internal Revenue Service 2009 Form 990.

Catalyst, Inc. 2008. U.S. Internal Revenue Service 2007 Form 990.

———. Catalyst Annual Report 2009. http://www.catalyst.org/etc/annual-reports/CATALYST_Annual_Report_2009-web.pdf.

———. Catalyst Member Benchmarking. http://www.catalyst.org/page/296/catalyst-member-benchmarking (accessed August 2, 2010).

———. Gender Stereotype Risk Assessment Toolkit (SRAT). http://www.catalyst.org/publication/354/catalyst-gender-stereotype-risk-assessment-toolkit-srat (accessed August 2, 2010).

———. Research & Knowledge. http://www.catalyst.org/page/52/research-knowledge (accessed August 2, 2010).

———. Types of Research & Knowledge.—http://www.catalyst.org/page/99/research-and-knowledge-types (accessed August 2, 2010).

Center for American Women and Politics, Eagleton Institute of Politics, Rutgers University. 2008. Record Number of Women to Serve in Senate and House. News release. November 5, 2008.

Center for American Women and Politics, Eagleton Institute of Politics, Rutgers University. 2008. *The Gender Gap*. New Brunswick: Center for American Women and Politics. http://www.cawp.rutgers.edu/fast_facts/voters/documents/GGPresVote.pdf.

———. National Information Bank on Women in Public Office.

———. *Summary of Women Candidates for Selected Offices 1970-2010 (Major Party Nominees)*. New Brunswick: Center for American Women and Politics. http://www.cawp.rutgers. edu/fast_facts/elections/documents/can_histsum.pdf.

Center for Women's Business Research. 2007a. Guide for Financing Business Growth Offers Actionable Advice for Women Business Owners. News release. April 4, 2007. http://www.womensbusinessresearch.com/press/details.php?id=156 (accessed July 27, 2010; web page no longer available).

———. 2007b. Security is Women Business Owners' Top Concern: Center for Women's Business Research & IBM Release Study Highlighting Technology Uses and Concerns. News release. June 20, 2007.

———. 2008. Biennial Update 2008: Businesses Owned by Women in the United States. http://www.sba.gov/advo/research/rs280tot.pdf.

———. 2009. The Economic Impact of Women-Owned Businesses in the United States. http://www.womensbusinessresearchcenter.org/Data/research/economicimpact stud/econimpactreport-final.pdf.

Child Trends. 2010. Percentage of Births to Unmarried Women 1960-2009. www.child trendsdatabank.org/?q=node/196 December, 2010. (accessed September 20, 2011.)

Commission of the European Communities. 2007 *Tackling the pay gap between women and men.* Brussels: Commission of the European Communities.

Committee on Gender Differences in the Careers of Science, Engineering, and Mathematics Faculty; Committee on Women in Science, Engineering, and Medicine; National Research Council. 2009. *Gender Differences at Critical Transitions in the Careers of Science, Engineering and Mathematics Faculty*. Washington, D.C: The National Academies Press.

CONSAD. 2009. *An Analysis of Reasons for the Disparity in Wages Between Men and Women* (Pittsburgh, 2009). Prepared for the U.S. Department of Labor.

Cornish, Mary. 2007. Closing the Global Gender Pay Gap: Securing Justice for Women's Work. *Comparative Labor Law and Policy Journal* 28 (2): 219.

Cortes, Patricia, and Jose Tessada. 2008. Cheap Maids and Nannies: How Low-Skilled Immigration is Changing the Labor Supply of High-Skilled American Women. Working Paper, Massachusetts Institute of Technology. http://www.iza.org/conference_files/TAM_08/cortes_p4231.pdf.

Croson, Rachel, and Uri Gneezy. 2009; Gender Differences in Preferences. *Journal of Economic Literature* 47 (2): 448–74.

DeAro, Jessie. 2010. Bringing Title IX to Classrooms and Labs. Blog post. The White House, Council on Women and Girls blog. June 24, 2010. http://www.whitehouse.gov/blog/2010/06/24/bringing-title-ix-classrooms-and-labs.

DeLeire, Thomas, and Helen Levy. 2001. *Gender, Occupation Choice and the Risk of Death at Work*. Working Paper No. 8574, National Bureau of Economic Research.

DeNavas-Walt, Carmen, Bernadette D. Proctor, and Jessica C. Smith. 2009. Income, Poverty, and Health Insurance Coverage in the United States: 2008. U.S. Census Bureau, Current Population Reports P60–236. Washington, D.C.: U.S. Government Printing Office.

Dey, Judy Goldberg and Catherina Hill. Behind the Pay Gap. *American Association of University Women Educational Foundation*. Washington, D.C.: American Association of University Women Educational Foundation, 2007.

Ellison, Glenn, and Ashley Swanson. 2010. The Gender Gap in Secondary School Mathematics at High Achievement Levels: Evidence from the American Mathematics Competitions. *Journal of Economic Perspectives* 24 (2): 109–28.

England, Paula. 2005. Gender Inequality in Labor Markets: The Role of Motherhood and Segregation. *Social Politics: International Studies in Gender, State and Society* 12 (2): 264–88.

Famighetti, Robert, ed. 1997. *The World Almanac and Book of Facts 1998*. Mahwah, New Jersey: St. Martins Press.

Feder, Jody, and Linda Levine. 2007. Pay Equity Legislation in the 110th Congress. CRS Report for Congress RL31867. Updated January 5, 2007. Washington, D.C.: Congressional Research Service.

Fox-Genovese, Elizabeth. 1996. *Feminism is Not the Story of My Life*. New York: Doubleday.

Francis, Roberta W. Frequently Asked Questions. http://www.equalrightsamendment.org/faq.htm (accessed July 29, 2010).

Furchtgott-Roth, Diana. 2010. Obama, Title IX, and Academics? Blog post, July 9, 2009. RealClearMarkets.com. http://www.realclearmarkets.com/articles/2009/07/09/obama_title_ix_and_academics__97300.html.

Glass Ceiling Commission. 2005. *Good for Business: Making Full Use of the Nation's Human Capital*. Washington, D.C.: U.S. Department of Labor.

Goldin, Claudia. 1991. The Role of World War II in the Rise of Women's Employment. *American Economic Review* 81 (4): 741–56.

———. 2002. *The Rising (and then Declining) Significance of Gender.* Working Paper No. 8915, National Bureau of Economic Research.

———. 2004a. *From the Valley to the Summit: The Quiet Revolution that Transformed Women's Work.* Working Paper No. 10335, National Bureau of Economic Research.

———. 2004b. The Long Road to the Fast Track: Career and Family." —*Annals of the American Academy of Political and Social Science* 596 (1): 20–35.

———. 2006. The Quiet Revolution that Transformed Women's Employment, Education, and Family. *American Economic Review* 96 (2): 1–21.

Goldin, Claudia, and Lawrence F. Katz. 2002. The Power of the Pill: Oral Contraceptives and Women's Career and Marriage Decisions. *Journal of Political Economy* 110 (4): 730–70.

———. 2008. Transitions: Career and Family Lifecycles of the Educational Elite. *American Economic Review.* 98 (2): 363–9.

Goldin, Claudia, Lawrence F. Katz, and Ilyana Kuziemko. 2006. The Homecoming of American College Women: The Reversal of the College Gender Gap. *Journal of Economic Perspectives* 20 (4): 133–56.

Grall, Timothy S. 2009. Custodial Mothers and Fathers and Their Child Support: 2007. Current Population Reports. Washington, D.C.: U.S. Census Bureau. http://www.census.gov/prod/2009pubs/p60-237.pdf.

Hill, M. Anne, and June O'Neill. 1992 An Intercohort Analysis of Women's Work Patterns and Earnings. In *Research in Labor Economics 13*, ed. Ronald Ehrenberg, 215–86. Greenwich, Connecticut: JAI Press.

Hisrich, Robert, and Candida Brush. 1984. The Woman Entrepreneur: Management Skills and Business Problems. *Journal of Small Business Management* 22 (1): 30–8.

"H.J.Res.61 – Proposing an amendment to the Constitution of the United States relative to equal rights for men and women." *OpenCongress.* July 29, 2010, http://www.open congress.org/bill/111-hj61/show.

Hotchkiss, Julie L., and M. Melinda Pitts. 2007. The Role of Labor Market Intermittency in Explaining Gender Wage Differentials. *American Economic Review* 97 (2): 417–21.

Hymowitz, Carol and Timothy D. Schellhardt. "The Corporate Woman (A Special Report): Cover–The Glass Ceiling: Why Women Can't Seem to Break the Invisible Barrier That Blocks Them From the Top Jobs." *Wall Street Journal.* 24 March 1986.

Ichino, Andrea, and Enrico Moretti. 2009. Biological Gender Differences, Absenteeism and the Earning Gap. *American Economic Journal: Applied Economics* 1 (1): 183–218.

International Confederation of Free Trade Unions. 2003. *Trade Union World Briefing. Equality through pay equity.* Brussels: International Confederation of Free Trade Unions.

International Labour Organization. 2004. *Breaking through the Glass Ceiling—Women in Management.* Geneva: International Labour Organization.

———. 2009. *Global Employment Trends for Women.* Geneva: International Labour Organization.

Johnson, Richard W., and Joshua M. Wiener. 2006. *A Profile of Frail Older Americans and Their Caregivers.* Washington, D.C.: The Urban Institute. http://www.urban.org/publications/311284.html.

Kephart, Pamela, and Lillian Schumacher. 2005. Has the "Glass Ceiling" Cracked? An Exploration of Women Entrepreneurship. *Journal of Leadership & Organizational Studies* 12 (1): 2–16.

Kleinjans, Kristin J. 2009. Do Gender Differences in Preferences for Competition Matter for Occupational Expectations? *Journal of Economic Psychology* 30 (5): 701–10.

Korn/Ferry Institute. 2008. 34th Annual Board of Directors Study. Los Angles, California: The Korn/Ferry Institute.

Levy, Helen. 2006. *Health Insurance and the Wage Gap*. Working Paper No. 11975, National Bureau of Economic Research.

Macpherson, David A., and Barry T. Hirsh. 1995. Wages and Gender Composition: Why Do Women's Jobs Pay Less? *Journal of Labor Economics* 13 (3): 426–71.

Mattis, Mary C. 2004. Women Entrepreneurs: Out From Under the Glass Ceiling. *Women in Management Review* 19 (3): 154.

Munasinghe, Lalith, Alice Henriques, and Tania Reif. 2008. The Gender Gap in Wage Returns on Job Tenure and Experience. *Labour Economics* 15. (6): 1296–316.

Murphy, Evelyn. 2005. *Getting Even: Why Women Don't Get Paid Like Men—and What to Do About It*. New York: Touchstone.

National Association of Women Business Owners. Key Facts About Women Business Owners and their Enterprises. *National Women's Business Council*. 22 September 2004.

National Organization for Women, Inc. 2009. U.S. Internal Revenue Service 2008 Form 990.

———. 2009. National NOW Conference Resolutions. http://www.now.org/organization/conference/resolutions/2009.html (accessed July 29, 2010).

———. Chronology of the Equal Rights Amendment, 1923–1996. http://www.now.org/issues/economic/cea/history.html (accessed July 29, 2010).

———. Frequently Asked Questions. http://www.now.org/organization/faq.html, (accessed July 29, 2010).

———. NOW and Constitutional Equality. *National Organization for Women*. http://www.now.org/issues/constitution/index.html (accessed July 29, 2010).

———. NOW and Economic Justice. http://www.now.org/issues/economic/index.html (accessed July 29, 2010).

———. Highlights from NOW's Forty Fearless Years. http://www.now.org/history/timeline.html (accessed July 29, 2010).

National Organization for Women Foundation, Inc. 2009. U.S. Internal Revenue Service 2008 Form 990.

National Women's Law Center. 2008a. A Platform For Progress: Building a Better Future for Women and Their Families. http://www.nwlc.org/pdf/PlatformforProgress2008.pdf (accessed August 2, 2010; page no longer available).

———. 2008b. U.S. Internal Revenue Service 2007 Form 990.

———. About the National Women's Law Center. http://www.nwlc.orgdisplay.cfm?section=About%20NWLC (accessed August 2, 2010; page no longer available).

Newman, Jody. 1997. The Gender Story: Women as Voters and Candidates in the 1996 Elections. In *America at the Polls 1996*, ed. Regina Dougherty, Evett C Ladd, David Wilber, and Lynn Zayachkiwsky,102 . Storrs, Connecticut: Roper Center for Public Opinion Research.

O'Neill, June. 1973. The Sex Differential in Earnings and Labor Market Discrimination Against Women. *Journal of Contemporary Business* (Summer): 41–52.

———. 1985. The Trend in the Male-Female Wage Gap in the United States. *Journal of Labor Economics* 3 (1): S91–S116.

———. 1991. The Wage Gap Between Men and Women in the United States. Women's Wages: Stability and Change in Six Industrialized Countries. In *International Review of Public Policy 3*, ed. S.L. Wilborn, (JAI Press; New York.) 353–69.

———. 1992. A Flexible Work Force: Opportunities for Women. *Journal of Labor Research* 13 (1): 67-72.

———. 2003. The Gender Gap in Wages, circa 2000. *American Economic Review* 93 (2): 309–414.

O'Neill, June, and Dave M. O'Neill. 2005. *What do Wage Differentials Tell us about Labor Market Discrimination?* Working Paper No. 11240, National Bureau of Economic Research.

O'Neill, June, and Solomon Polachek. 1993. Why the Gender Gap in Wages Narrowed in the 1980s. *Journal of Labor Economics* 2 (1): 205–28.

Organisation for Economic Co-operation and Development. 2008. *Higher Education to 2030.* Vol. 1, *Demography*. Paris, France: Organisation for Economic Co-operation and Development.

———. 2009. *SF2.1: Fertility Rates. OECD Family Database*. Paris, France: Organisation for Economic Co-operation and Development.

———. 2011. *OECD Family Database.* Paris, France: Organisation for Economic Co-operation and Development.

———. 2011. *OECD Family Database. Doing Better for Families.* Paris, France: Organisation for Economic Co-operation and Development.

———. OECD Database 2011, Education at a Glance, 2011 OECD Indicators. http://www.oecd.org/dataoecd/61/2/48631582.pdf.

Paringer, Lynn. 1983. Women and Absenteeism: Health or Economics? In *Papers and Proceedings of the Ninety-Fifth Annual Meeting of the American Economic Association, American Economic Review* 73 (2): 123–.27.

Pearson, Eric. 2010. *National Review: Benching the Title IX Changes*. News story, June 1, 2010. National Public Radio. http://www.npr.org/templates/story/story.php?storyId=127306783.

Rhode, Deborah. 1997. *Speaking of Sex: The Denial of Gender Inequality*. Cambridge, Massachusetts: Harvard University Press.

Robinson, John, and Geoffrey Godbey. 1997. *Time for Life: The Surprising Ways Americans Use their Time*. University Park, Pennsylvania: Pennsylvania State University Press.

Shang, Qingyan, and Bruce Weinberg. 2009. *Opting for Families: Recent Trends in the Fertility of Highly Educated Women*. Working Paper No. 15074, National Bureau of Economic Research.

Shelton, Lois M. 2006. Female Entrepreneurs, Work Family Conflict, and Venture Performance: New Insights into the Work-Family Interface. *Journal of Small Business Management* 44 (2): 285–98.

Small, D.A., L. Babcock, M. Gelfand, & H. Gettman (2003, November). Gender and the initiation of negotiations in ambiguous situations. Paper presented at the annual meeting of the Society for Judgment and Decision Making, Vancouver, British Columbia, Canada.

Taylor, Paul, et al., *The Rising Age Gap in Economic Well-Being*, Pew Research Center, 2011.

Tosi, Henry L., and Steven W. Einbender. 1985. The Effects of the Type and Amount of Information in Sex Discrimination Research: A Meta-Analysis. *The Academy of Management Journal* 28 (3): 712–23.

U.S. Bureau of the Census. 1976. *Historical Statistics of the United States. 1926*, vol. 1 1975, series B28-35, 52. http://www2.census.gov/prod2/statcomp/documents/CT1970p1-01.pdf.

———. 2001. *Survey of Women-Owned Businesses 1997.*

———. 2002. *Survey of Business Owners—Women-Owned Firms.* http://www.census.gov/econ/sbo/02/womensof.html.

———. 2009a. *American's Families and Living Arrangements.*

———. 2009b. *Men's and Women's Earnings by State. 2008 American Community Survey.*

———. 2010. *USA Quick Facts.* Revised April 22, 2010. http://quickfacts.census.gov/qfd/states/00000.html (accessed July 27, 2010).

———. 2011 *Statistical Abstract of the United States. The National Data Book.* http://www.census.gov/compendia/statab/cats/labor_force_employment_earnings.html.

U.S. Centers for Disease Control and Prevention. 1988. National Center for Health Statistics. *National Vital Statistics Report 1985.*

———. *Health, United States 2008.* 2009.

———. *National Vital Statistics Report 2009.* 2011.

U.S. Department of Education. 2010. National Center for Education Statistics. Institute of Education Sciences. *Digest of Education Statistics 2009.*

U.S. Department of Education. Office of Civil Rights. 2003. *Further Clarification of Intercollegiate Athletics Policy Guidance Regarding Title IX Compliance.* Issued July 11, 2003. http://www2.ed.gov/about/offices/list/ocr/title9guidanceFinal.html.

U.S. Department of Labor. Bureau of Labor Statistics. 1999. *Current Employment Statistics: Employment and Earnings.*

———. 2008a. *Labor Force Characteristics by Race and Ethnicity.* <http://www.bls.gov/cps/cpsrace2008.pdf.

———. 2008b. *Highlights of Women's Earnings in 2007.*

———. 2009a. *Highlights of Women's Earnings in 2008.*

———. 2009b. *Women in the Labor Force: A Databook.* Report 1018.

———. 2010a. *Current Employment Statistics: Employment and Earnings.*

———. 2010b. *Highlights of Women's Earnings in 2009.*

———. 2010c. *Labor Force Characteristics by Race and Ethnicity 2009.*

———. 2010d. *National Census of Fatal Occupational Injuries in 2009.*

———. 2010e. *Women in the Labor Force: A Databook.*

———. 2011. *Current Employment Statistics: Employment and Earnings.*

———. *Current Population Survey.*

———. *Establishment Survey.*

U.S. Department of Labor. Bureau of Labor Statistics. Division of International Labor Comparisons. *International Comparisons of Annual Labor Force Statistics, Adjusted to U.S. Concepts, 10 Countries, 1970-2010.*

U.S. Equal Employment Opportunity Commission. 2004. *Indicators of Equal Employment Opportunity. Labor Force Characteristics by Race and Ethnicity.*

———. Employer Information Reports (EEO-1 Single and Consolidated Reports).

U.S. Government Accountability Office. 2001. *Women in Management: Analysis of Selected Data from the Current Population Survey.* Congressional Briefing Slides.

———. 2009. *Women's Pay: Converging Characteristics of Men and Women in the Federal Workforce Help Explain the Narrowing Pay Gap.*

U.S. Small Business Administration. Office of Advocacy. 2006. *Women in Business: 2006. A Demographic Review of Women's Business Ownership.* http://www.sba.gov/advo/research/rs280tot.pdf.

U.S. Statutes. *Health Care and Education Reconciliation Act of 2010.*

———. 2007. The Facts on SBA Loans to Minorities and Women 2007. News release, May 9, 2007. http://www.sba.gov/news/pressmain/index.html.

Waldfogel, Jane. 1989. Working Mothers Then and Now: A Cross-Cohort Analysis of the Effects of Maternity Leave on Women's Pay. In *Gender and Family Issues in the Workplace*, ed. Francine D. Blau and Ronald G. Ehrenberg, 92-126. New York: Russell Sage Foundation.

———. 2006. *What Children Need.* Cambridge, Massachusetts: Harvard University Press.

Weiler, Stephan, and Alexandra Bernasek. 2001. Dodging the Glass Ceiling? Networks and the New Wave of Women Entrepreneurs. *The Social Science Journal* 38 (1): 85–103.

Weinberger, Catherine, and Peter Kuhn. 2006. *The Narrowing of the U.S. Gender Earnings Gap, 1969–1999: A Cohort-Based Analysis.* Working Paper No. 12115, National Bureau of Economic Research.

Women's Vote Watch. 2008. Gender Gap Evident in the 2008 Election: Women, Unlike Men, Show Clear Preference for Obama over McCain. News release, November 5, 2008. http://www.cawp.rutgers.edu/press_room/news/documents/PressRelease_ 11-05-08_womensvote.pdf.

World Economic Forum. 2007. *Global Gender Gap Report.* Geneva: World Economic Forum.

Index

About the Author

*D*iana Furchtgott-Roth is a senior fellow at the Manhattan Institute for Policy Research. She is the author of *How Obama's Gender Policies Undermine America* (Encounter Books, 2010) and editor of *Overcoming Barriers to Entrepreneurship in the United States* (Rowman and Littlefield, 2008). Together with Christine Stolba, she authored the first edition of *Women's Figures: An Illustrated Guide to the Economic Progress of Women in America* (AEI Press, 1999), and *The Feminist Dilemma: When Success Is Not Enough* (AEI Press, 2001).

Ms. Furchtgott-Roth was senior fellow at Hudson Institute from 2005 to 2011. Prior to that, she served as chief economist of the U.S. Department of Labor. From 2001 to 2002 she served as chief of staff of the President's Council of Economic Advisers under President George W. Bush. Ms. Furchtgott-Roth served as Deputy Executive Director of the Domestic Policy Council and Associate Director of the Office of Policy Planning in the White House under President George H.W. Bush from 1991 to 1993, and she was an economist on the staff of President Reagan's Council of Economic Advisers from 1986 to 1987.

Ms. Furchtgott-Roth is contributing editor for RealClear Markets.com and an economics columnist for *The Examiner*. She writes a monthly column on tax issues for *Tax Notes*. She appears regularly on TV and radio to comment on economic policy.

Ms. Furchtgott-Roth received her B.A. in economics from Swarthmore College and her M.Phil. in economics from Oxford University.

Jeremy A. Rabkin
Professor of Law
George Mason University
School of Law

Richard J. Zeckhauser
Frank Plumpton Ramsey Professor
of Political Economy
Kennedy School of Government
Harvard University

Research Staff

Ali Alfoneh
Resident Fellow

Joseph Antos
Wilson H. Taylor Scholar in Health
Care and Retirement Policy

Leon Aron
Resident Scholar; Director,
Russian Studies

Paul S. Atkins
Visiting Scholar

Michael Auslin
Resident Scholar

Claude Barfield
Resident Scholar

Michael Barone
Resident Fellow

Roger Bate
Resident Scholar

Walter Berns
Resident Scholar

Andrew G. Biggs
Resident Scholar

Edward Blum
Visiting Fellow

Dan Blumenthal
Resident Fellow

John R. Bolton
Senior Fellow

Karlyn Bowman
Senior Fellow

Alex Brill
Research Fellow

Charles W. Calomiris
Visiting Scholar

Lynne V. Cheney
Senior Fellow

Steven J. Davis
Visiting Scholar

Mauro De Lorenzo
Visiting Fellow

Sadanand Dhume
Resident Fellow

Thomas Donnelly
Resident Fellow; Director,
AEI Center for Defense Studies

Mackenzie Eaglen
Resident Fellow

Nicholas Eberstadt
Henry Wendt Scholar in
Political Economy

Jon Entine
Visiting Fellow

Rick Geddes
Visiting Scholar

Jonah Goldberg
Fellow

Christopher A. Gorry
Research Fellow

Scott Gottlieb, M.D.
Resident Fellow

Kenneth P. Green
Resident Scholar

Michael S. Greve
John G. Searle Scholar

Kevin A. Hassett
Senior Fellow; Director,
Economic Policy Studies

Steven F. Hayward
F. K. Weyerhaeuser Fellow

Robert B. Helms
Resident Scholar

Arthur Herman
NRI Visiting Scholar

Frederick M. Hess
Resident Scholar; Director,
Education Policy Studies

Ayaan Hirsi Ali
Visiting Fellow

R. Glenn Hubbard
Visiting Scholar

Frederick W. Kagan
Resident Scholar; Director,
AEI Critical Threats Project

Karthik Kalyanaraman
NRI Fellow

Leon R. Kass, M.D.
Madden-Jewett Chair

Andrew P. Kelly
Research Fellow

J.D. Kleinke
Resident Fellow

Desmond Lachman
Resident Fellow

Adam Lerrick
Visiting Scholar

Lawrence B. Lindsey
Visiting Scholar

John H. Makin
Resident Scholar

Aparna Mathur
Resident Scholar

Lawrence M. Mead
Visiting Scholar

Thomas P. Miller
Resident Fellow

Charles Murray
W. H. Brady Scholar

Roger F. Noriega
Fellow

Stephen D. Oliner
Resident Scholar

Norman J. Ornstein
Resident Scholar

Pia Orrenius
Visiting Scholar

Richard Perle
Resident Fellow

Mark J. Perry
Scholar

Tomas J. Philipson
Visiting Scholar

Edward Pinto
Resident Fellow

Alex J. Pollock
Resident Fellow

Vincent R. Reinhart
Visiting Scholar

Richard Rogerson
Visiting Scholar

Michael Rubin
Resident Scholar

Sally Satel, M.D.
Resident Scholar

Gary J. Schmitt
Resident Scholar; Director,
Program on American Citizenship

Mark Schneider
Visiting Scholar

David Schoenbrod
Visiting Scholar

Nick Schulz
DeWitt Wallace Fellow;
Editor-in-Chief, American.com

Roger Scruton
Visiting Scholar

Sita N. Slavov
Resident Scholar

Kent Smetters
Visiting Scholar

Vincent Smith
Visiting Scholar

Christina Hoff Sommers
Resident Scholar; Director,
W. H. Brady Program

Michael R. Strain
Research Fellow

Phillip Swagel
Visiting Scholar

Erin Syron
NRI Fellow

Marc A. Thiessen
Fellow

Stan A. Veuger
NRI Fellow

Alan D. Viard
Resident Scholar

Peter J. Wallison
Arthur F. Burns Fellow in
Financial Policy Studies

David A. Weisbach
Visiting Scholar

Paul Wolfowitz
Scholar

John Yoo
Visiting Scholar

Benjamin Zycher
NRI Visiting Fellow